Heavy Metal Riffs for Guitar.

by Mark Michaels.

Amsco Publications
New York/London/Sydney/Cologne

Photo Credits
pages 13, 22, 23, 26, 30, 38, 39, 44, 47, 51, 66, 67, 68 (right),
74, 82, 85, 89, 91, 94, 96, 98, 99 (bottom), 100: *Ebet Roberts*
page 17 (top): *Richard Chang*
page 57: courtesy *Atlantic Records*

Amsco Publications has conducted an exhaustive search to locate the
photographers or copyright owners of the photographs in this
book. However, in the event that we have inadvertently published a
copyrighted photograph without proper acknowledgement, we advise
the copyright owner to contact us so that we may give appropriate
credit in future editions.

Photo research by Valerie Boyd and Louise Moed
Biographical text by Curtis Cates
Book design by Margo Dittmer
Cover design by Pearce Marchbank
Edited by Peter Pickow

International Standard Book Number: 0.8256.2329.4

Exclusive Distributors:
Music Sales Corporation
24 East 22nd Street, New York, NY 10010 USA
Music Sales Limited
8/9 Frith Street, London W1V 5TZ England
Music Sales Pty. Limited
27 Clarendon Street, Artarmon, Sydney NSW 2064 Australia

Printed in the United States of America by
Vicks Lithograph and Printing Corporation

CONTENTS

PREFACE

In the current musical world of stylish production and synthesizer-technology dominance, Heavy Metal remains true to the power and feeling originally associated with Rock and Roll. Though seen as being anachronistic by its detractors, Heavy Metal's worldwide popularity attests to its vitality today. True, the image of the "hard rocker" hasn't changed much over the decades, but while the thrust of the music remains largely the same as always, the style of guitar has changed in leaps and bounds.

Heavy Metal Riffs for Guitar brings guitar into the 1980s by examining and notating many of the riffs which are closely identified with this genre. In a sense, it picks up on an area left untouched by my previous *Rock Riffs* and *Blues Riffs for Guitar*. I have included musical examples which are illustrative of some of the new riffs you hear on records, and have purposely avoided pentatonic (blues-box fingering) hammering-on and pulling-off riffs, "Chuck Berry-type" riffs and other cliches for this reason. Some of the new areas we'll explore are the use of the unmeasured tremolo, bimanual (two-handed) riffs, chromatic and diminished riffs, and bitonality (mixing two keys). The book is roughly graded so you should be able to progress easily from the first few examples right through to the end. Special solo sections are included, from your favorite hard-rock pieces.

Def Leppard, Van Halen, Iron Maiden, Night Ranger, Ozzy O., Quiet Riot, Rush, Judas Priest, Scorpions, Triumph, and Gary Moore (among many others) all had a hand in preparing this book. The music and riffs of these great bands have been an inspiration for me in writing *Heavy Metal Riffs* as well as in my own playing. The experience of researching this book proved to me that those who dismiss this entire musical style without really getting to know it firsthand do music in general a great disservice, and subject many fine guitarists to unfair prejudices. Heavy Metal is no more or less repetitive than any other genre, and from my knowledge this includes Rock, Jazz, Blues, Folk, Country, and Classical.

There is much to be learned from careful study and practice of the riffs in this book. It can open up for you, the beginning or intermediate/advanced guitarist, new ways of thought in approaching your instrument. All of the material presented is available on cassette tape from the *Riff Series Companion*, for which an order blank appears on the last page. Keep practicin', good luck, and ROCK ON!

SYMBOLS AND NOTATION

⊓	downstroke
V	upstroke
>	accent
∿∿∿	heavy vibrato
⟋	slide up
⟍	slide down
♪	harmonic (notation)
◇12	harmonic (tablature)
tr	trill
PO	pulloff
H	hammeron
BU	bend up
BD	bend down
SL	slide
PSL	pick, then slide
SLP	slide, then pick
ML	mute with left hand
MR	mute with right hand
MLR	mute with left and right hands
R	fret with right-hand finger
8va	play an octave higher than written

When notes are written inside parentheses, they are to be fingered but not played. I use this notation to show which fret to finger when bending notes. Notes that are not to be bent but are also within parentheses are ghost notes, which may or may not be played.

Half-Note and Eighth-Note Riffs

Listen to Quiet Riot's "Slick Black Cadillac" (from *Metal Health*) to hear a riff like the following one.

This riff, similar to what Glenn Tipton plays on Judas Priest's "Bloodstone," uses a single motif repeated in three different octaves.

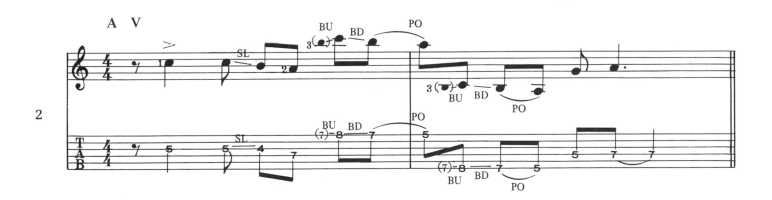

The introduction to Judas Priest's "Screaming for Vengeance" features a riff like this one.

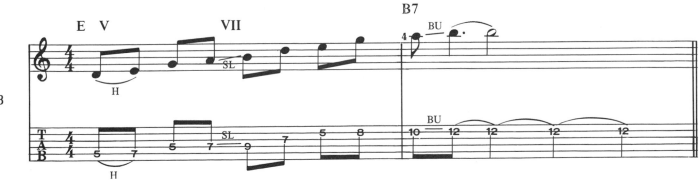

See how the notes from a D major scale are used against an E major chord.
Refer to Van Halen's "Atomic Punk."

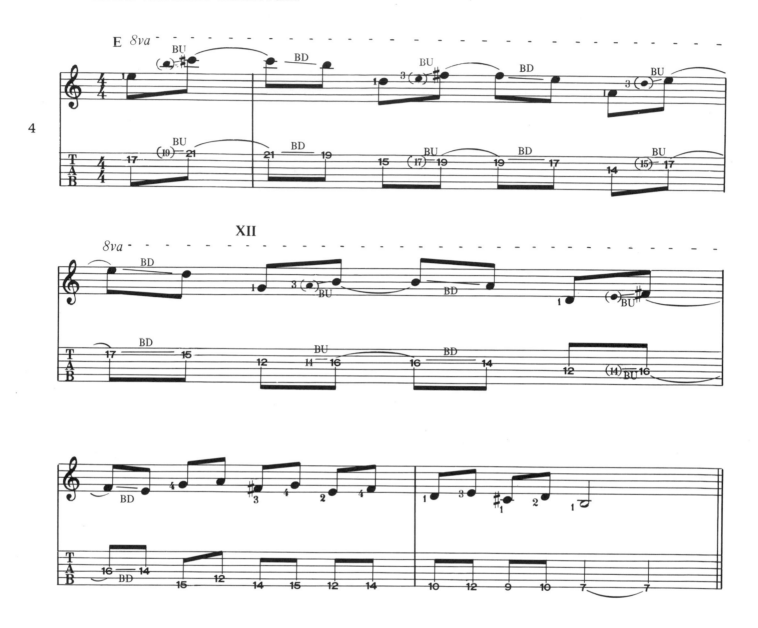

Rik Emmett plays a riff similar to this one in Triumph's "Allied Forces,"
on the album of the same name.

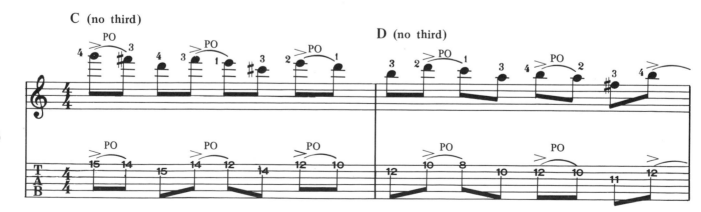

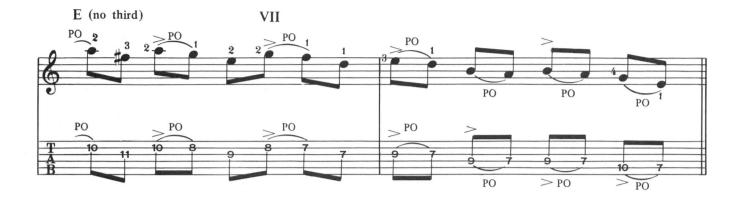

Note the use of the flatted fifth (A♭) in this riff. Listen to Alex Lifeson on Rush's "Free Will."

Check out the flatted fifth in the third measure of this riff, similar to what is played in Rush's "Digital Man" on *Signals.* The melody here is quite ear-catching.

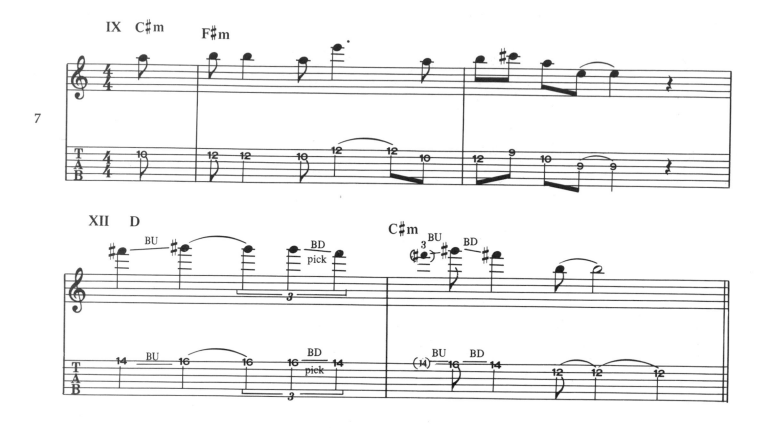

Listen to Foghat's "Stone Blue" to hear riffs like the following two:

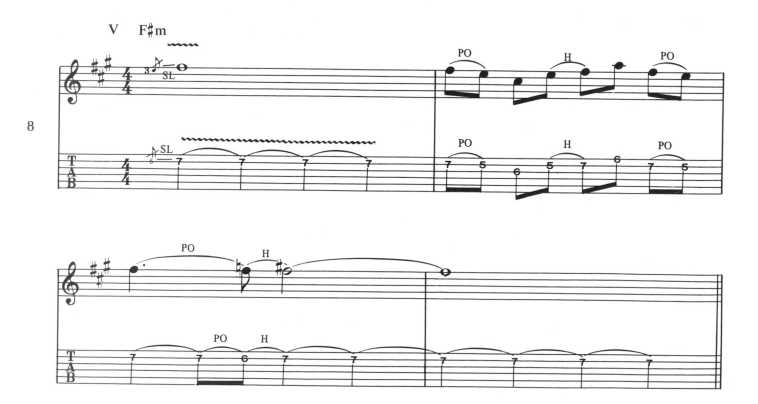

10

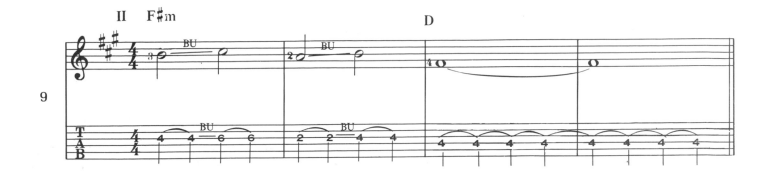

The motif in the first two measures here is repeated up a whole step in the third and fourth measures, to go along with the chord change. Refer to AC/DC's "Let There Be Rock."

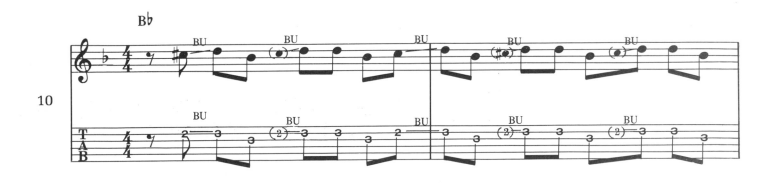

Here's a neat way to arpeggiate chords, very reminiscent of Ritchie Blackmore's playing on Deep Purple's "Burn."

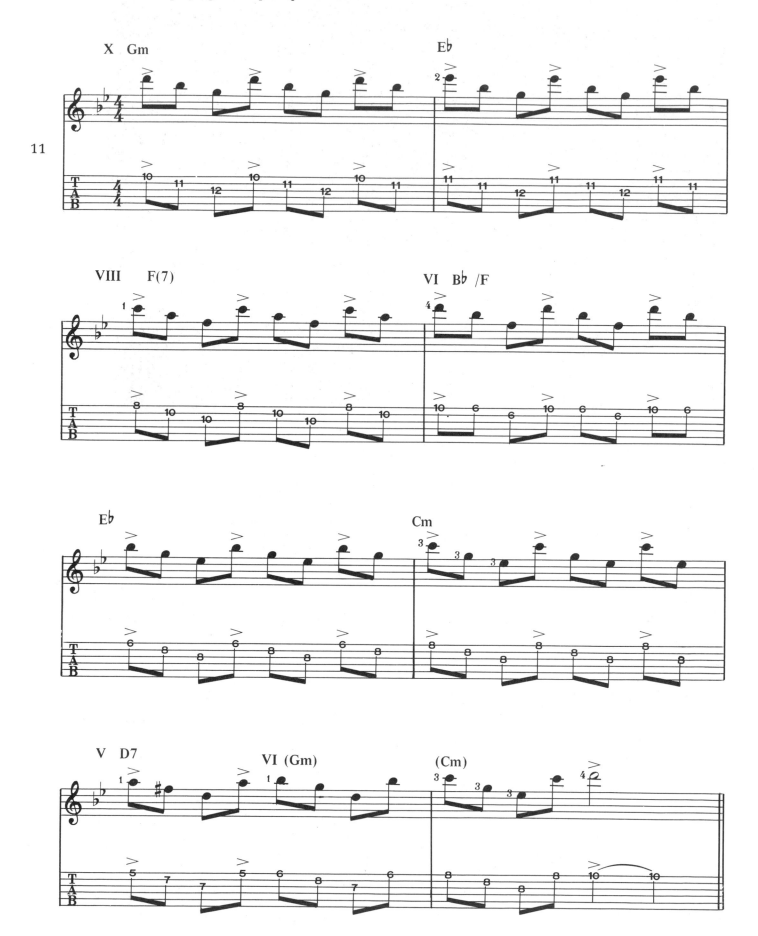

Foghat

Listen to Judas Priest's "Fever" to hear a riff like the following:

Special Solo Section:
AC/DC's "You Shook Me All Night Long"

This solo, similar to the well known solo by Angus Young of AC/DC, is notable for its simplicity and construction. In spite of a limited choice of notes, mostly from the A blues (C Pentatonic) scale, Young's powerful attack, sparse phrasing, and heavy vibrato turn an otherwise uneventful solo into an emotional tour de force.

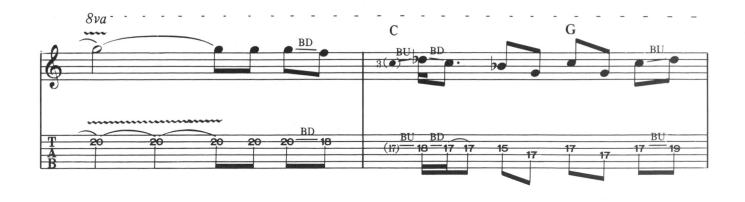

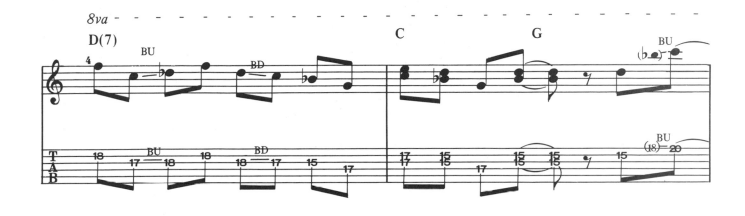

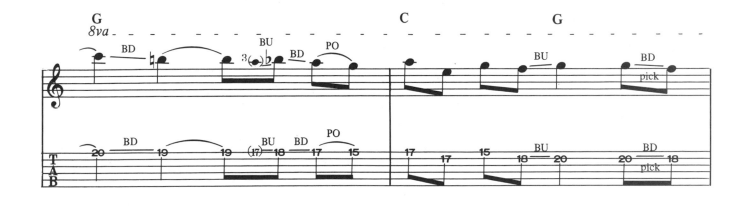

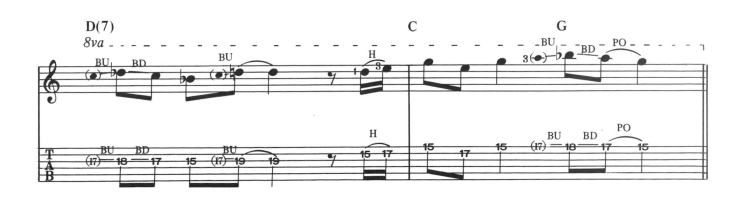

Alex Lifeson

Alex Lifeson feels that inventing guitar parts that emphasize and characterize the meaning of the lyrics is his role as guitarist for Canada's Rush. Lifeson has outgrown the need to be a fast guitarist and instead concentrates on building guitar parts that will stand the test of time.

Early in Rush's career Lifeson began experimenting with guitar synthesizer and Moog bass in an effort to expand the band in a musically progressive direction. Lifeson sees the role of the guitar in Rush as that of one instrument in the ensemble, and not the most important one. Rush is not a guitar band, but a band that utilizes various instruments as a means toward an end. His use of guitar is getting away from flurries of notes and moving toward a more rhythmic approach.

Lifeson continually edits his playing, listening back and utilizing studio tapes, portable four-track studios, and cassettes of sound checks. His solos show the effect of this self evaluation. Hours of listening back to himself play makes for a much more structured style than that of a player who continually improvises.

Currently Lifeson uses Strats and Teles and prefers the Roland Jazz Chorus amp with its built-in chorus effect. Lately he has been experimenting with the whammy bar on the Stratocaster. Combining this technique with his formidable array of unusual effects, such as a Harminicomputer and a Korg DDL, produces his distinctive sound. No matter what sounds, effects, or parts you hear on Rush's records, you can be sure that Lifeson will attempt to duplicate them live—anything for the fans.

Alex Lifeson, Neil Peart, and Geddy Lee: Rush

Triplet Riffs: Two Measures Long

Check out Def Leppard's "Die Hard the Hunter" (from *Pyromania*) to hear a riff similar to the following one:

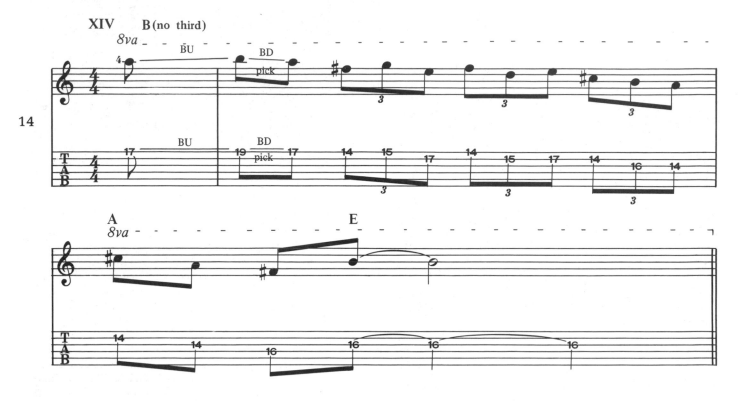

Randy Rhoads's solo in Ozzy Osbourne's "Tonight" features a riff similar to this one.

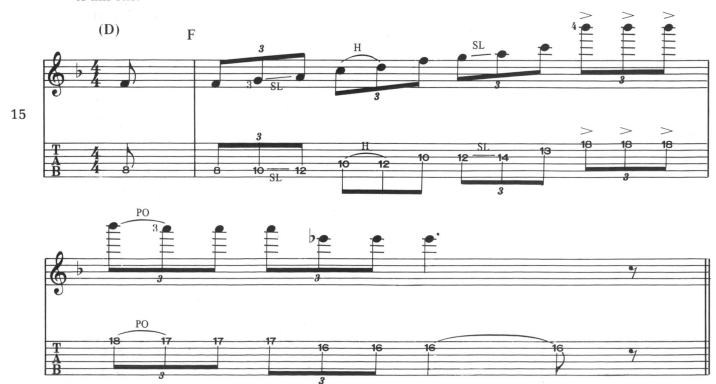

Refer to the Scorpions' "Blackout" to hear a fill like this one.

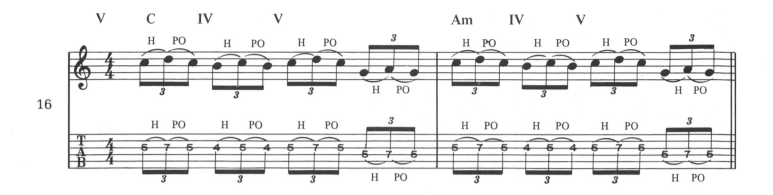

This riff, similar to what Michael Schenker plays in his solo on the Scorpions' "Now!," features the flatted fifth interval.

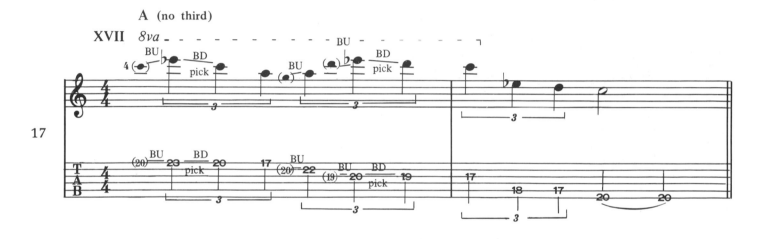

To get an idea of how the following two riffs sound, listen to Foghat's "Honey Hush" from *Foghat Live!*

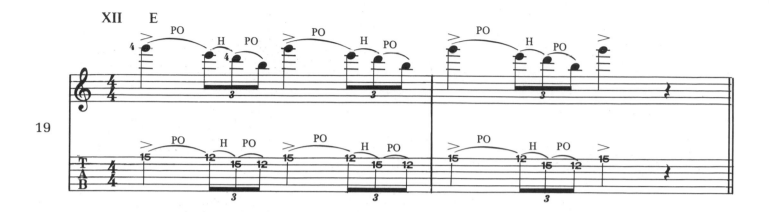

Listen to Judas Priest's "Electric Eye" to hear a riff like this one.

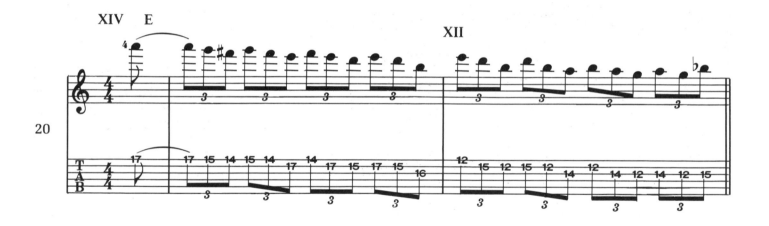

Refer to "Take These Chains" by Judas Priest.

The C major scale is appropriate for playing over both the Bm7♭5 chord as well as the Dm chord. Listen to Def Leppard's "Billy's Got a Gun" from *Pyromania*.

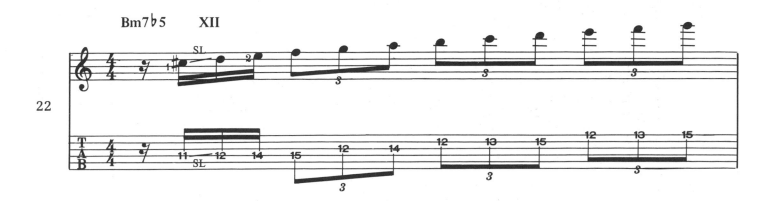

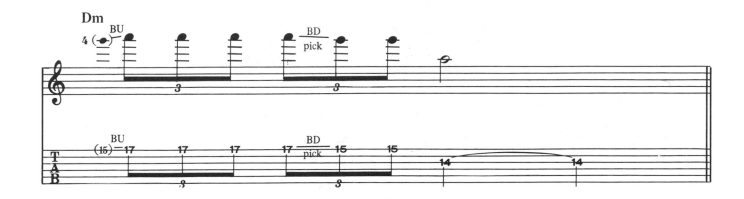

This riff is very similar to what is played on Def Leppard's "Bringin' on the Heartbreak" from *High n' Dry*.

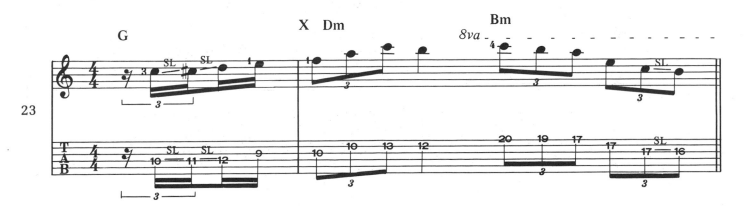

Michael Schenker

Michael Schenker began his musical career earning one deutschemark for each Beatle song he could figure out and teach his older brother Rudolf, guitarist for the Scorpions. Born in 1955, in Sarstedt, West Germany, Michael began teaching himself guitar at the age of nine and by age eleven was performing with his first band, Enervates. With the personal goal of being able to play without thinking, Michael began practicing four to eight hours a day in his mid teens. At age sixteen he made his recording debut on the Scorpions' *Lonesome Crow*. In 1973, at the age of eighteen he was asked to join UFO. He contributed to four UFO albums, then quit upon the completion of 1979's double LP *Strangers in the Night* after finding it difficult to express his creativity. In 1979, after a brief reunion of the Scorpions to record *Lovedrive*, Michael formed his own band, the Michael Schenker Group.

Schenker's trademark is his black and white 1970 Gibson Flying V which he has had since he was sixteen. On stage he goes through a Cry Baby wah-wah and 50-watt Marshall amps. He admits that he doesn't "know the names of all those effects in the studio."

Michael Schenker is considered one of the giants of European Heavy Metal guitarists. His playing combines melodic hooks and full chords with fast runs and harmonics to carry his musical ideas in new directions. His lack of formal musical training has not detered him from expanding his playing style.

Triplet Riffs: Three Measures Long

You'll have to stretch your fourth (pinky) finger a bit in order to properly execute this riff. Refer to Iron Maiden's "Hallowed Be Thy Name" from *Number of the Beast*.

24

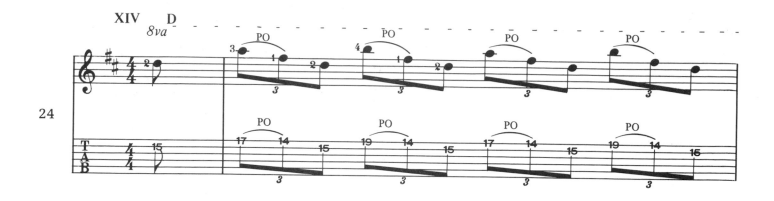

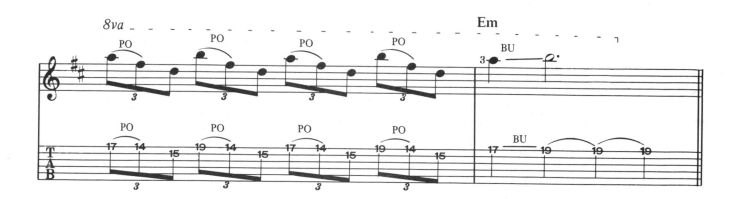

Listen to Rik Emmett's playing on Triumph's "Allied Forces" to hear a riff just like this one.

25

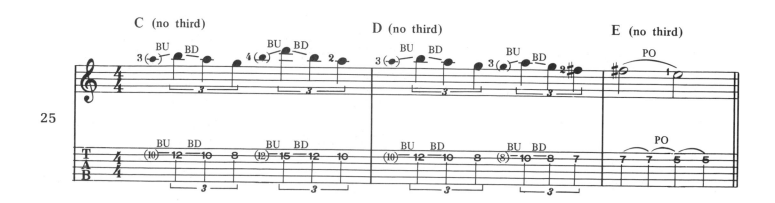

This riff is played over a shuffle beat, which explains the dotted eighth-notes at the outset. Refer to Deep Purple's "Hold On" featuring Ritchie Blackmore.

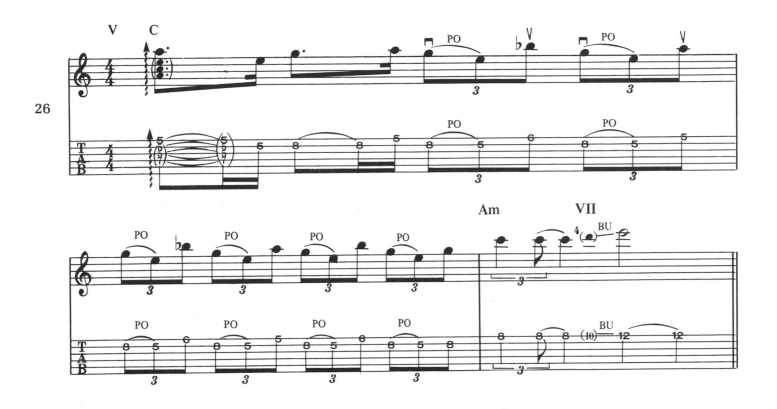

The following riff is reminiscent of David Gilmour's playing on his solo album.

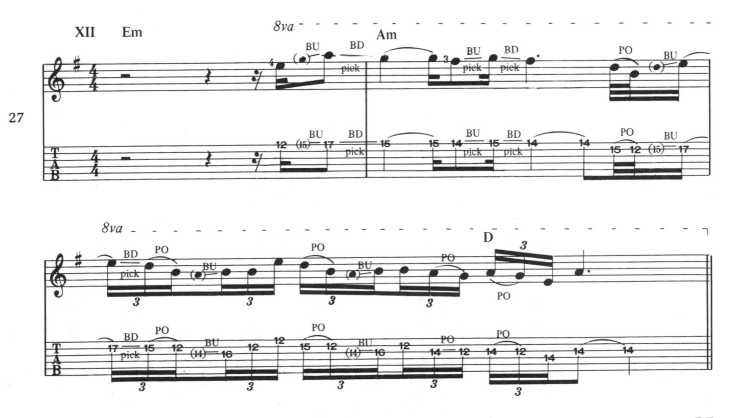

Iron Maiden

Scorpions

Triplet Riffs: Four Measures Long

Def Leppard's "Wasted" (from *Pyromania*) features a riff like this one.

Combining triplets with eighth-notes gives this lick a different rhythmic feel. Refer to Iron Maiden's "The Prisoner."

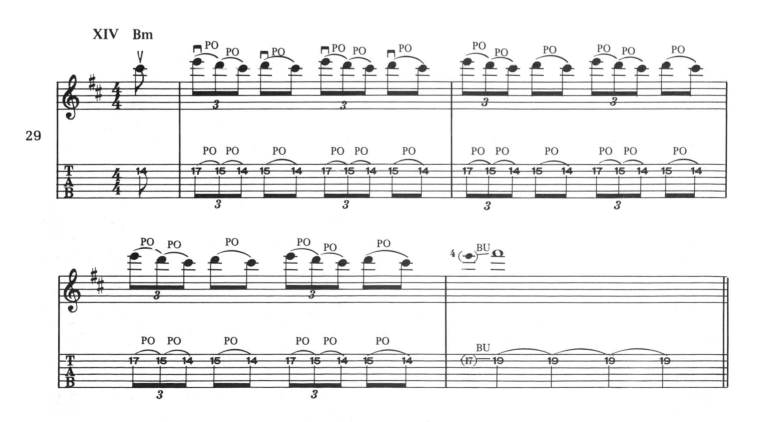

Listen to Van Halen's "Atomic Punk" for this kind of riff.

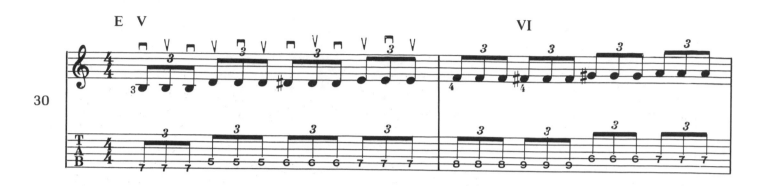

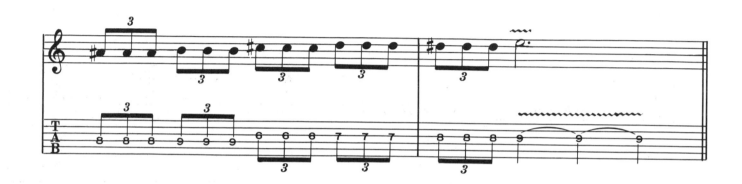

Note the use of the flatted fifth here, as in Judas Priest's "Electric Eye."

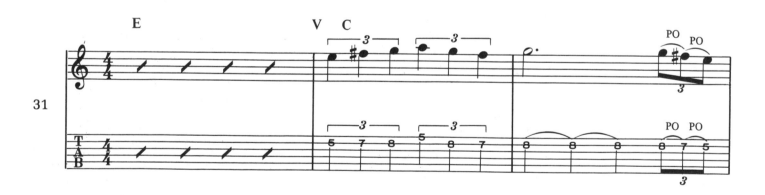

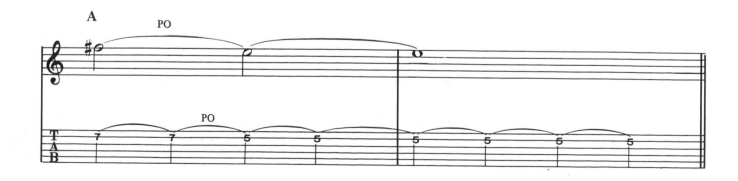

This qualifies as a triplet riff although it is notated in eighth notes because of the $\frac{12}{8}$ time signature. Refer to Iron Maiden's "Quest for Fire."

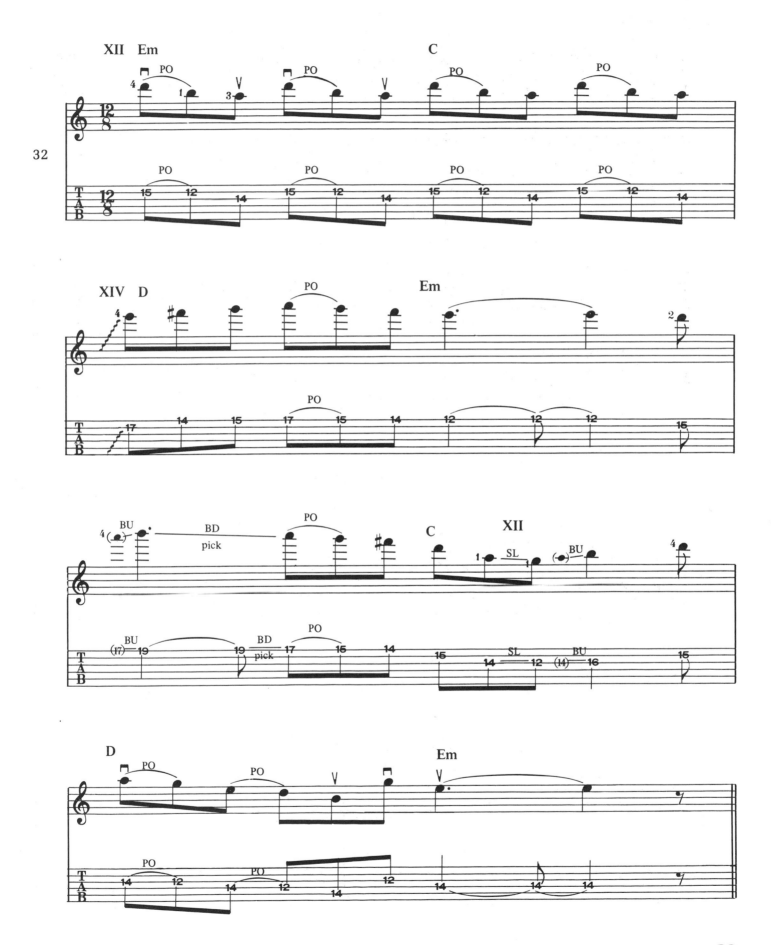

Eddie Van Halen

"What I put into it, it gives me back." That quote from Eddie Van Halen best sums up his relationship with guitar playing. A fiercely dedicated professional, Eddie has been playing guitar since his brother, Alex, switched to drums. Born the son of a jazz reed player in 1957 in Nijmege, the Netherlands, Eddie moved to Pasadena, California in 1968 and formed his first Rock-and-Roll band, Mammoth. In 1976 Eddie and Alex formed Van Halen, incorporating Heavy Metal's most quotable and zany frontman, David Lee Roth. Success soon followed when Gene Simmons of Kiss saw them perform at California's Starwood Club and recommended them to Warner Brothers' president, Mo Ostin.

Eddie has what would probably be considered the most amazing hands of any guitarist—Heavy Metal or otherwise. He practically wrote the book on many of the techniques that are so popular with today's guitarists, such as right-hand hammering-on, tremolo-bar technique, and bimanual string-pulls. His vocabulary of bizarre noises is inexhaustible, and are all done without effect pedals. Eddie loves to play the guitar and does so constantly, before and after his shows. Eddie considers Eric Clapton his main influence and can play practically any Cream solo note-for-note.

Eddie's red Strat-style guitar with its black-and-white stripes is every bit as bizarre as some of the sounds he makes with it, including a neck from one, a body from another and pickups that are practically falling out. (Actually, only the treble pickup is wired in.) The guitar has only one volume knob and no tone control. In true Heavy Metal style, Eddie pumps his sound out through six 100-watt Marshall heads each feeding into bottoms of eight twelve-inch speakers. He has a full rack of effects which he claims never works. As a result he most often employs simple tape-delay set for a slow repeat. Due to Eddie's tremendous popularity, Kramer now markets a copy of his guitar, with the pickups a little more intact.

Special Solo Section: Van Halen's "Eruption"

This unaccompanied solo, similar to Van Halen's solo on "Eruption," is done entirely on the second (B) string and is played with both hands in the *bimanual* or "Van Halen" style. Begin by plucking the string while fingering the C♯, hammer on the E at the fifth fret with your (left) pinky, hammer the G♯ with your (right) index finger (*i*) and, to complete the pattern, again "pluck" or pull off with your right index finger, sounding the C that begins the sequence again.

Van Halen plays this solo without any reference to time in terms of number of measures; he just riffs until he riffs something different.

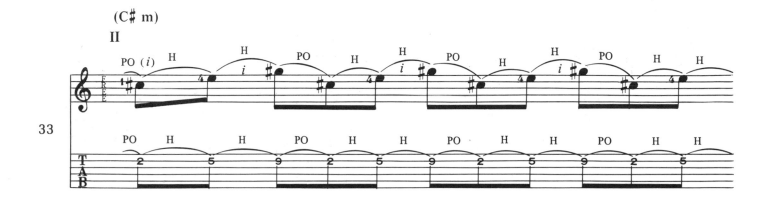

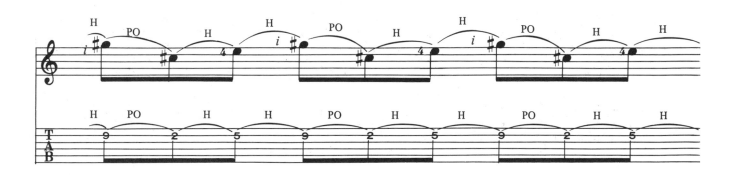

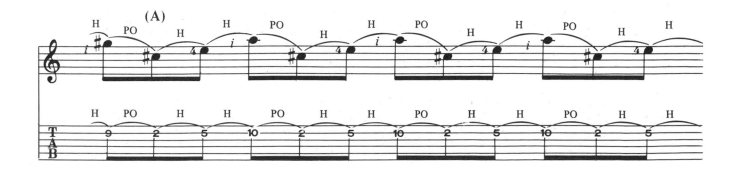

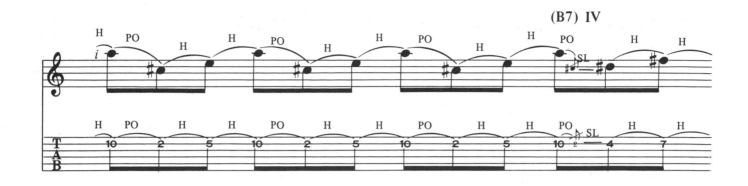

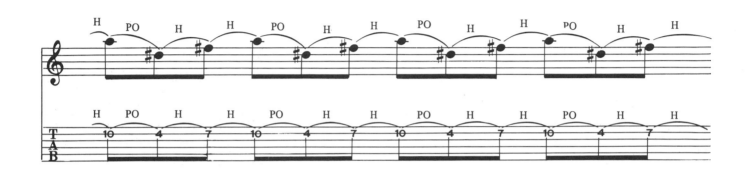

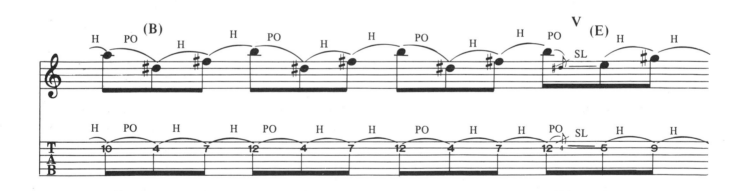

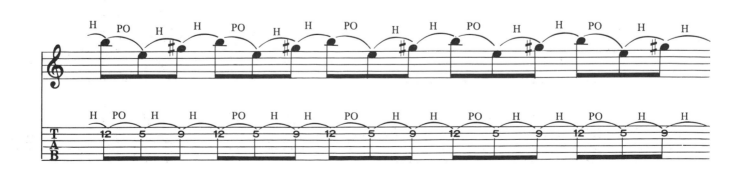

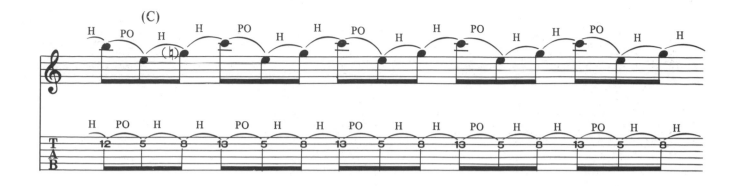

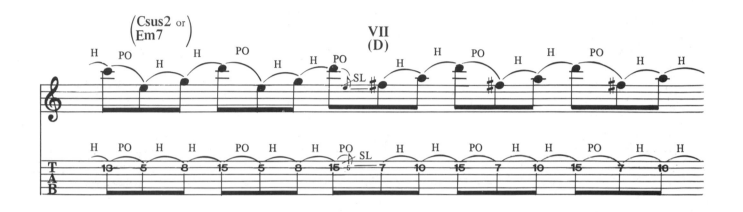

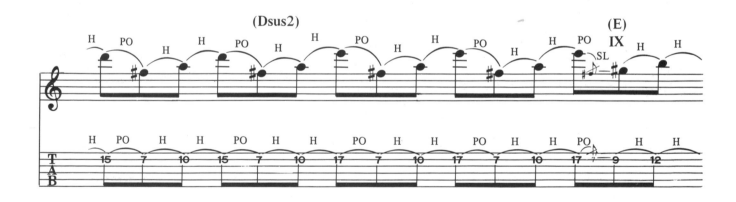

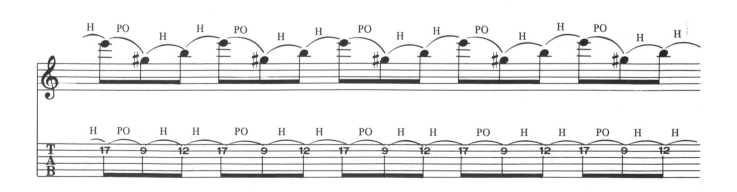

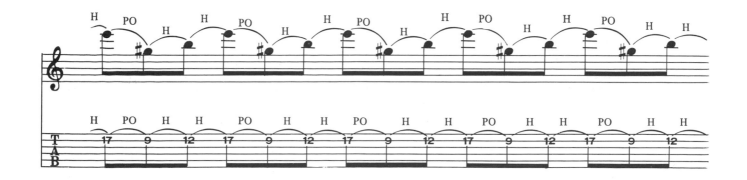

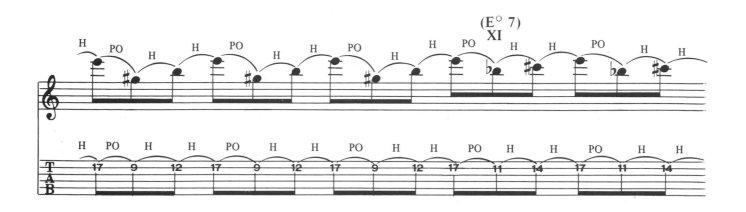

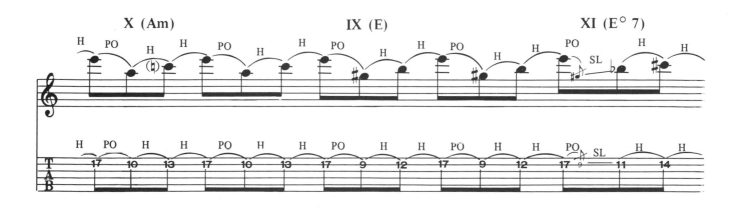

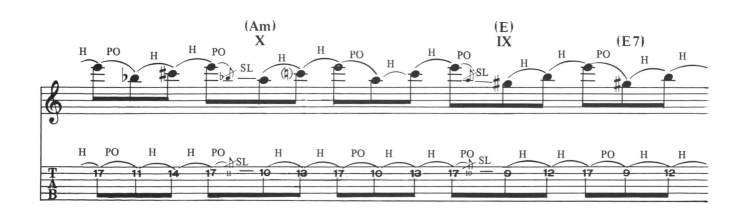

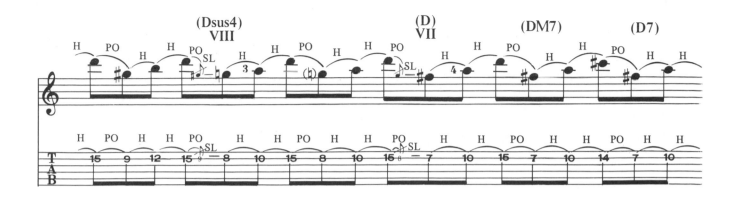

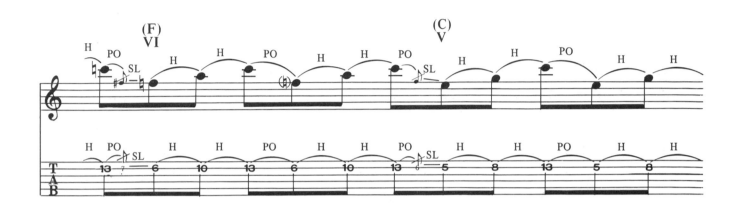

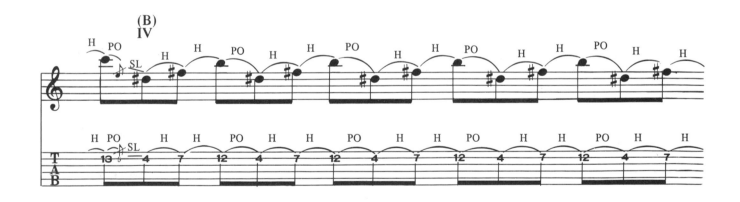

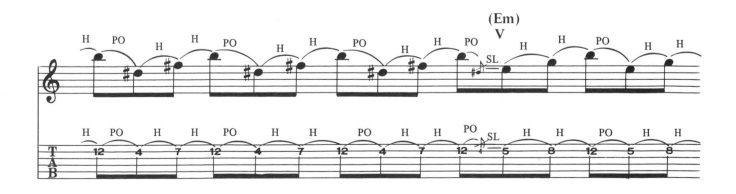

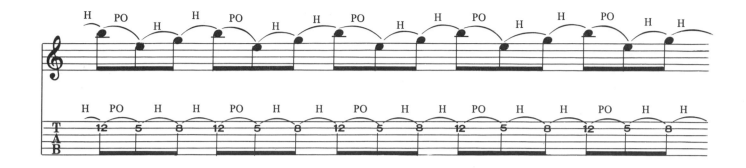

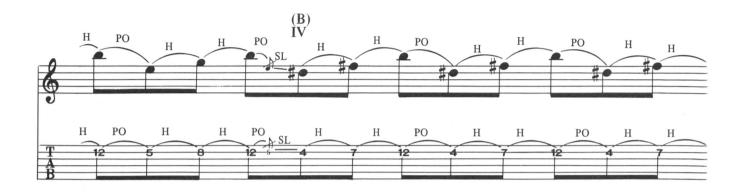

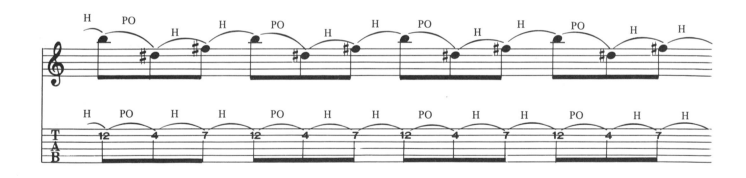

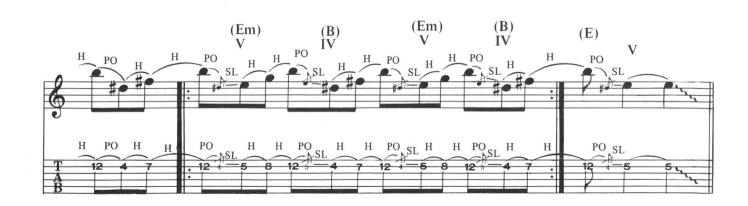

Glenn Tipton

Glenn Tipton, one of the guitarists for England's Judas Priest, states that Heavy Metal songs are the most difficult in the world to write. With that in mind it's easy to see why Judas Priest claim they put more energy into songwriting than touring. Tipton feels that guitar playing is a matter of feel and, even though he is a trained pianist, puts more emphasis on feeling than studying. In other words, reading music stunts your inventiveness and forces you to play what is written.

Tipton is an original member of Judas Priest, a band that was formed in the industrial city of Birmingham, England. Emerging in 1973 with their death-and-destruction theme, Judas Priest was a fusion of Blues and Heavy Metal. The band was signed by CBS in 1977 and has made vast improvement in both their recorded sound and their ability to play live since their early seventies independent LPs.

Tipton feels no need to practice guitar since Judas Priest maintains a constant touring schedule. He is influenced by the Beatles, Jimi Hendrix, Peter Green, Robert Johnson, as well as many current bands that he listens to in his spare time. He feels that players should realize a certain point in their playing where they drop their influences and channel everything into their own style.

Tipton uses both a Gibson SG and a new Fender Stratocaster with two Dimarzio Super Distortion pickups. The SG is basically a Standard but with the smaller neck of a Special. The guitar he uses in the studio is a 1961 Stratocaster which he keeps at home. The tone controls on all of his axes are disengaged and he uses the treble pickup exclusively. Glenn uses Ernie Ball picks and Guild Strings (gauges: .009, .009, .014, .022, .034, .038). His amp setup consists of two Marshall heads (one 50 and one 100-watt) into 4x12 bottoms. In his effects loop, either his custom-made treble boost or his MXR Distortion + is always on. Other effects in line include overdrive, a flanger, Phase 100, digital delay, a twelve-band graphic EQ, and a Maestro Echoplex.

Tipton prefers to stick to the recorded versions of his solos and tries to incorporate melody into metal. He is not a big fan of scales and so one hears more emphasis on feeling than on scale-study in a Glenn Tipton solo.

K.K. Downing and Glenn Tipton

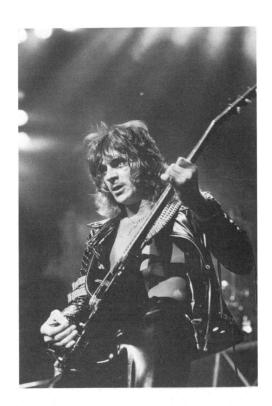

Downing, Rob Halford, and Tipton

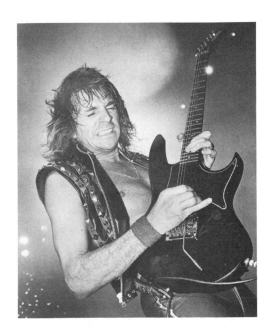

Sixteenth-Note Riffs: One Measure Long

This riff is pentatonic, played off of the blues-scale (box) fingering. Refer to REO's "Keep On Lovin' You."

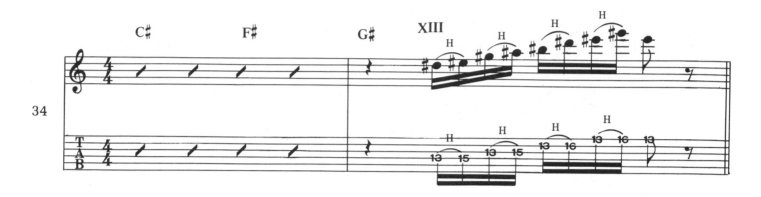

Listen to AC/DC's "Rock and Roll Ain't Noise Pollution" to get an idea of how this riff should sound.

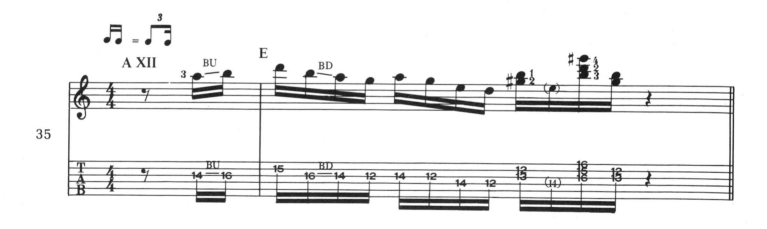

I sometimes execute this riff by picking the upstrokes with my (right) middle or ring finger. Listen to Foghat's "Fool for the City."

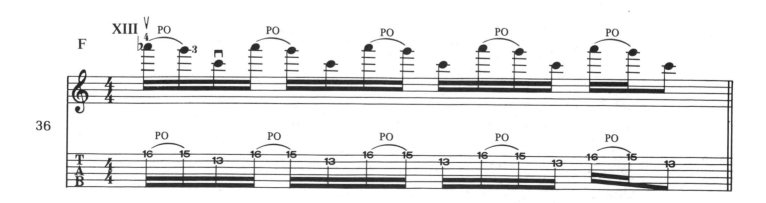

40

Sixteenth-Note Riffs: Two Measures Long

You should master this riff in all keys and positions before trying more complicated riffs of this kind.

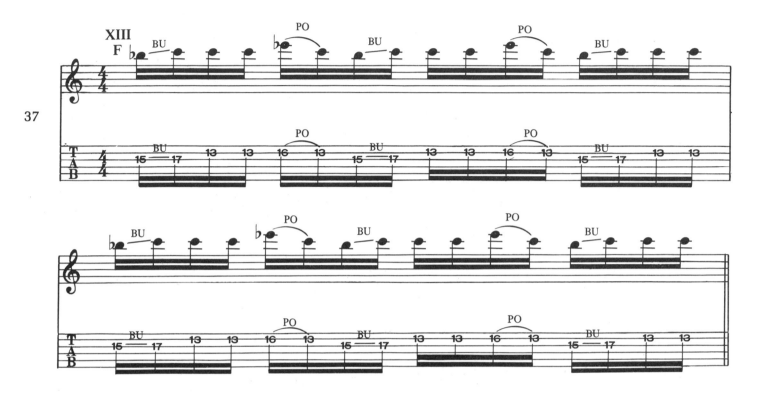

This lick is similar to what's played in Def Leppard's "Rock of Ages."

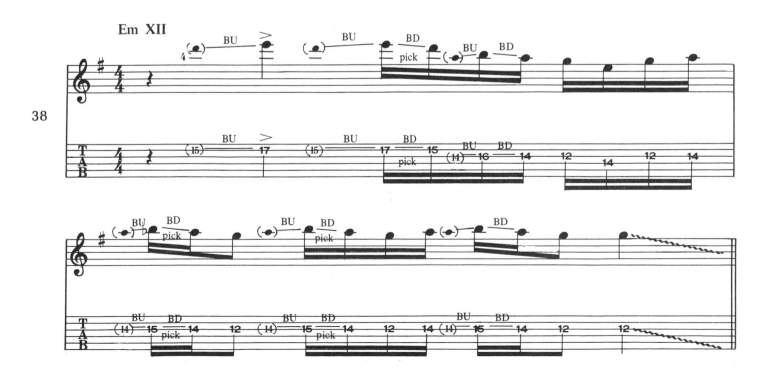

Compare the similarity of phrasing in the next two riffs. The first is like
Def Leppard's "You Got Me Runnin' " and the second sounds like Iron
Maiden's "Flight of Icarus" solo.

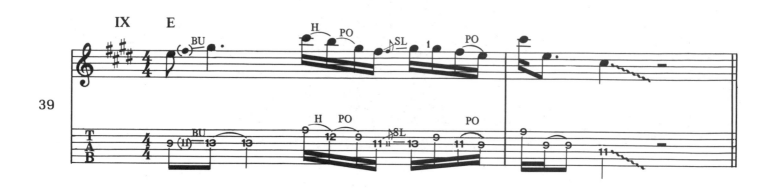

Check out Randy's use of E♭ (from the B♭ scale) and E natural (from the F
scale) against the Dm chord. Refer to "Mr. Crowley."

Angus Young of AC/DC plays something just like this in "Let Me Put My Love into You."

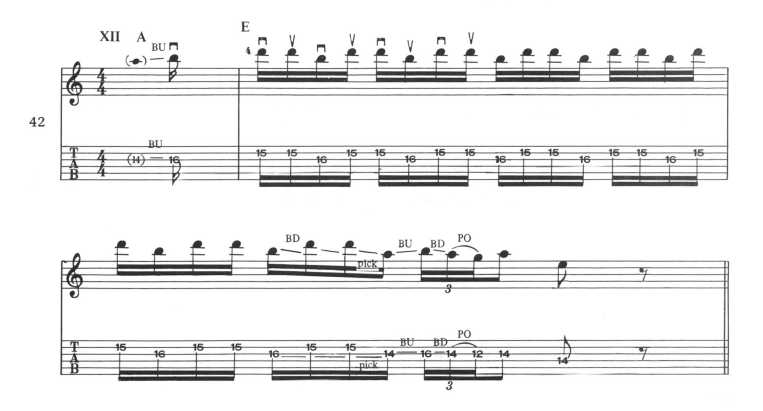

In Night Ranger's "Penny" (from *Dawn Patrol*) you'll hear pretty much these same two riffs. This is an excellent example of playing what is essentially the same riff two different ways: first as a partial chord and then as a pulloff/hammeron sequence.

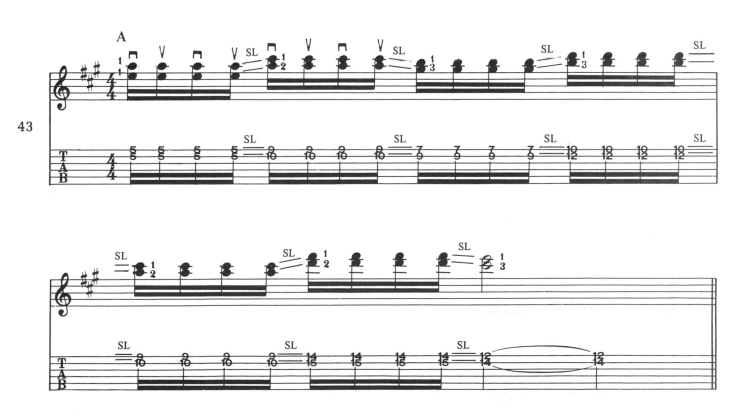

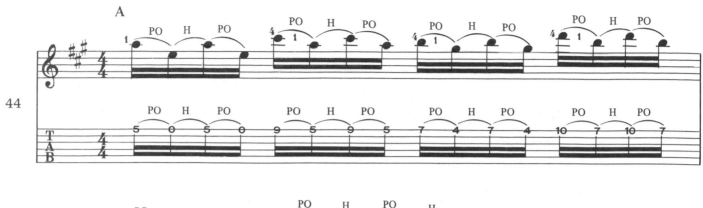

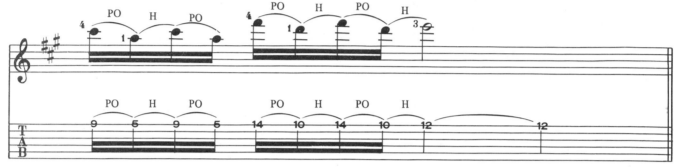

Quiet Riot's "Breathless" solo features this kind of riff, performed by the very exciting Carlos Cavazo.

Scorpions

Whether the technique used to play this riff is called *tremolo* or just "fast picking" doesn't really matter. Refer to "Now!" by the Scorpions from their *Blackout* album.

This riff has a country sound to it. Check out Jabs's playing on the Scorpions' "Arizona."

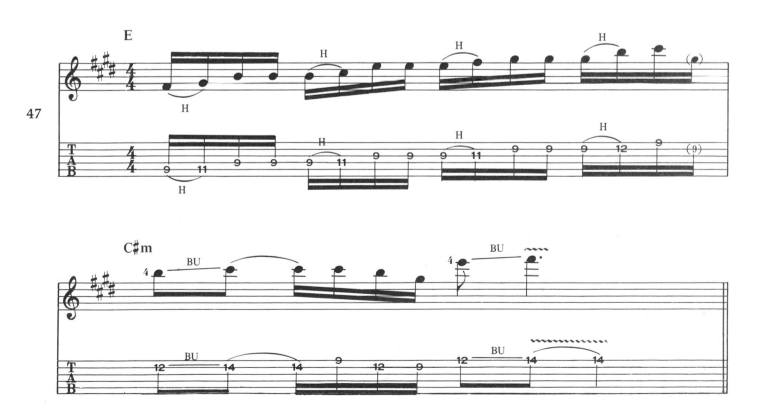

At the end of his solo in "YYZ," you'll hear Alex Lifeson of Rush play a riff like the following:

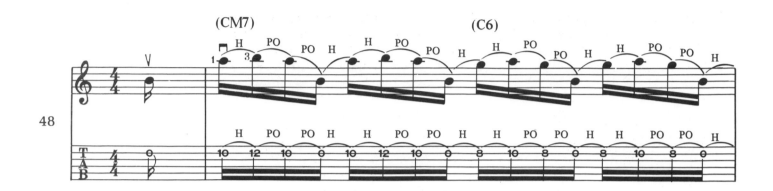

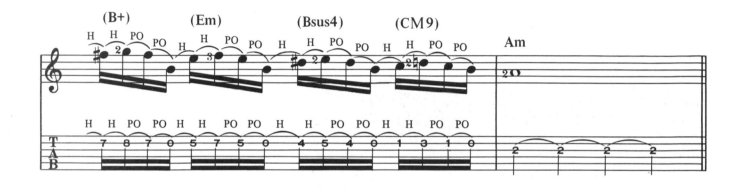

The end of "Diary of a Madman" features Randy Rhoads playing a lick like this one.

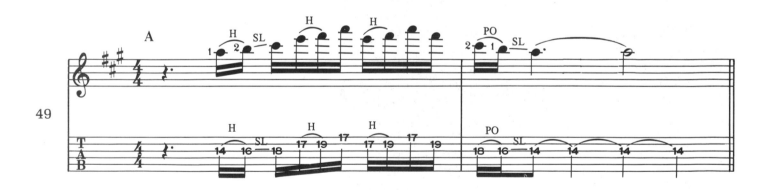

Ritchie Blackmore

Possibly the tastiest of all Heavy Metal guitarists is Ritchie Blackmore. Born in Weston-super Mare, England, Blackmore scored his first American hit in 1968 with "Hush" by Deep Purple. A look at Blackmore's influences and it's easy to see where his tasty style developed from: Duane Eddy, James Burton, Scotty Moore, and Big Jim Sullivan (whom he later studied with). While his influences may reflect the past, his style; utilizing tremolo-bar, hammering on, and finger-style picking; influences the current trend in guitar playing.

With a player like Blackmore, feeling is everything and the way he personally feels before going onstage generally affects his playing. Blackmore took Classical lessons for a year, claiming it helped him to develop his left hand, especially the use of his little finger, over the last few years. Blackmore has been using Strato-casters through Marshall stacks (he prefers small amps but finds he can't get the power rumble with them) and a Hornby-Skues variable treble boost for sustain. Blackmore suggests to starting players to get a good instrument and instruction book and copy licks from everybody: "Just steal."

Sixteenth-Note Riffs: Four Measures Long

Listen to Night Ranger's "At Night She Sleeps" to hear a riff very similar to this one.

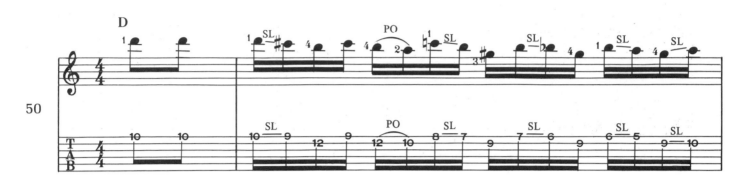

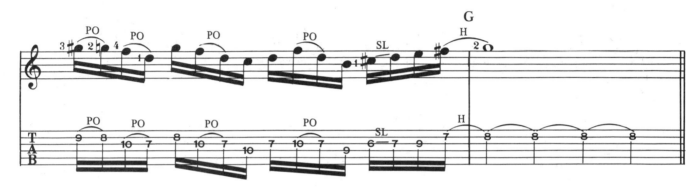

This riff comes out of the Randy Rhoads vocabulary; refer to his playing on Ozzy Ozbourne's "I Don't Know."

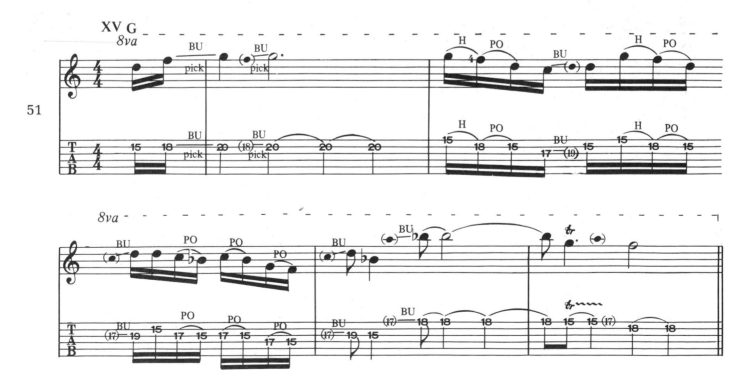

You will have to practice this slowly at first to get all of the phrasing and articulations correct. Check out Iron Maiden's "Ides of March" from *Killers* to hear how this can be played.

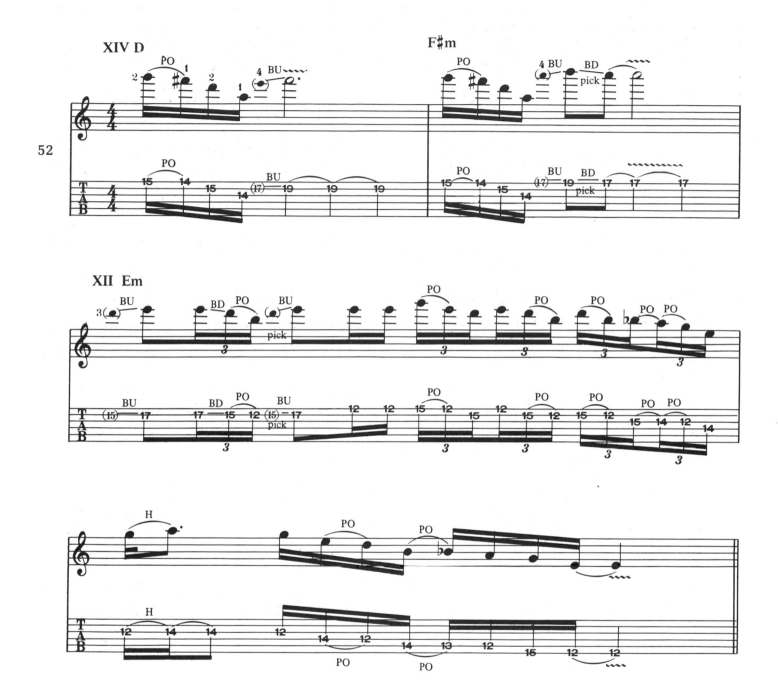

Carlos Cavazo

Carlos Cavazo, of Quiet Riot, recommends that beginning players learn as much about music as they can and suggests *Artful Arpeggios* by Don Mock and Ted Greene's *Chord Chemistry* as being very beneficial to him even though he is considered a Heavy Metal guitarist. He states that studying Classical music and learning to read music has helped him break the misconception that Heavy Metal is nonmusical. His solos combine tasty melodic riffing with strange diminished scales.

Quiet Riot utilized MTV to help them become one of the most successful Heavy Metal bands to debut ever, but it was a long haul getting to the top. The band was formed in Miami, Florida in the early seventies by lead singer Kevin Dubrow who expanded the line up in 1975 to include ace guitarist Randy Rhoads (who later left to tour and record with Ozzy Osbourne and, tragically, died in a plane crash). Cavazo was recruited to replace Rhoads from an L.A. Heavy Metal band called Snow, and Quiet Riot's first LP for a US label—*Metal Health*—was recorded. (This album has been one of the most successful Heavy Metal albums ever, selling 680,000 units in a single week.)

When Cavazo joined Quiet Riot, he was encouraged to play his own style rather than to try to copy Rhoads. At the time he joined the band he was already an accomplished player. Born in Atlanta in 1958 and raised in Orange and California counties in California, Cavazo started playing guitar at age eight and at age ten took two years of lessons where he learned Classical stylings and how to read music. He quit lessons and started playing and learning with friends, copying tunes and licks from the Beatles, Jeff Beck, and Jimi Hendrix (who was his main influence). In high school he started a band, with his brother on bass, called Speed of Light. After this band came Snow, in 1978, which was very popular on the L.A. club circuit and, in fact, opened some shows for the original Quiet Riot. Snow broke up in 1982 and two weeks later Dubrow called Cavazo and asked him to join Quiet Riot.

Today Cavazo may be seen playing any of several guitars including a black Washburn A-20V, a cream-colored early 70s Gibson Flying V, a Charvel Telecaster built by Grover Jackson, a Sunburst Falcon, and a black Washburn Eagle. His standard battery of effects is made up of a Vox Cry Baby wah-wah pedal, a Zeus distortion unit (which he leaves on all the time), a Boss Delay, a Boss Chorus, an MXR ten-band equalizer and a Washburn phase shifter.

Advanced Triplet and Sixteenth-Note Riffs

This riff is close to what Gary Moore plays in "Gonna Break My Heart Again" from *Corridors of Power*.

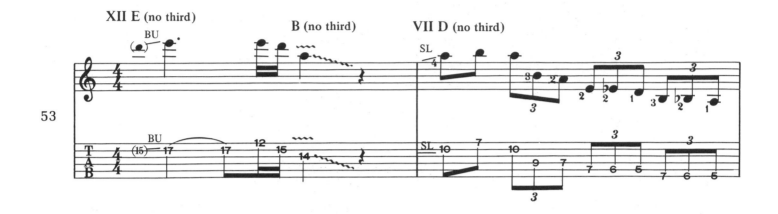

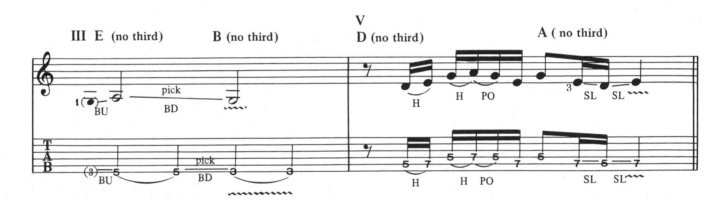

In Def Leppard's "Rock of Ages" you'll hear a riff like this one:

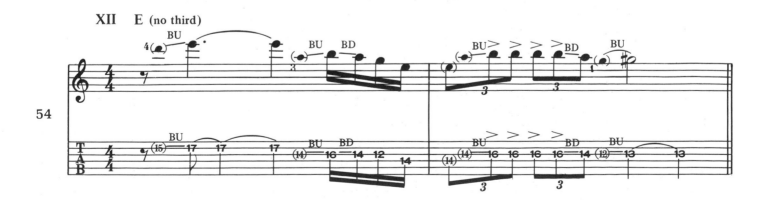

Here's another bluesy lick in the style of Angus Young. Listen to "Back in Black" to hear his interpretation of it.

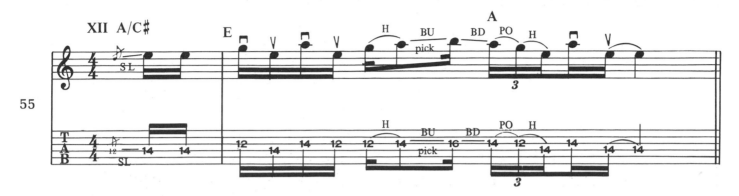

Practice this one slowly at first, unless you have Randy Rhoads's technique. Refer to "Goodbye to Dee" from the *Blizzard of Oz* album.

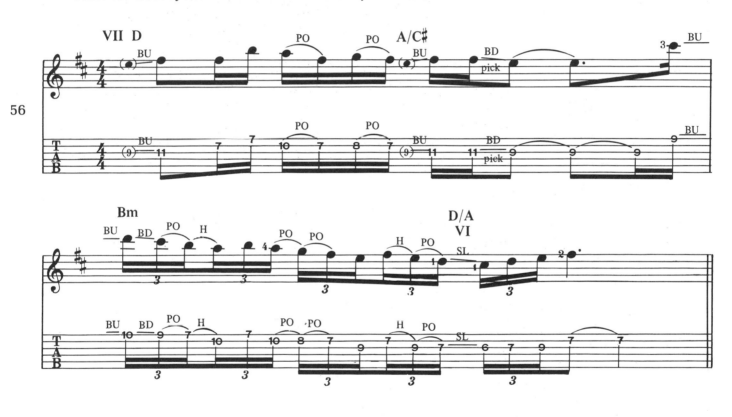

This riff uses some interesting intervals (♭5, ♭9) and comes very close to a riff in Def Leppard's "Answer to the Master" from *High n' Dry*.

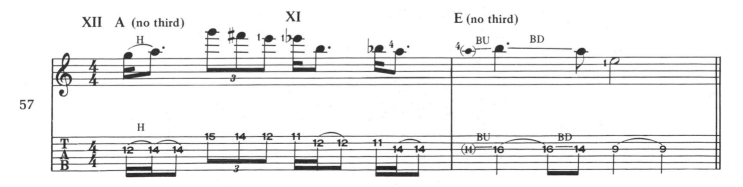

Here's an example of using notes from a G major scale against an A chord
(with or without a third). Refer to Iron Maiden's "Invaders," from *Number
of the Beast*.

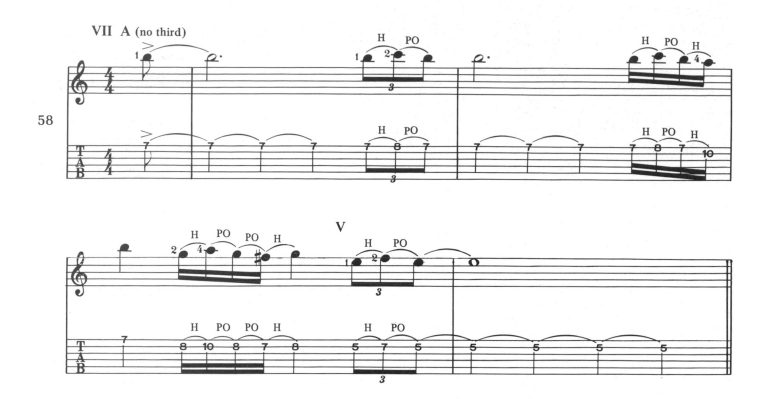

Rather than combining sixteenth notes with eighth-note triplets, this riff
consists of sixteenth-note triplets. Refer to AC/DC's "Shake a Leg" with
Angus Young riffing out.

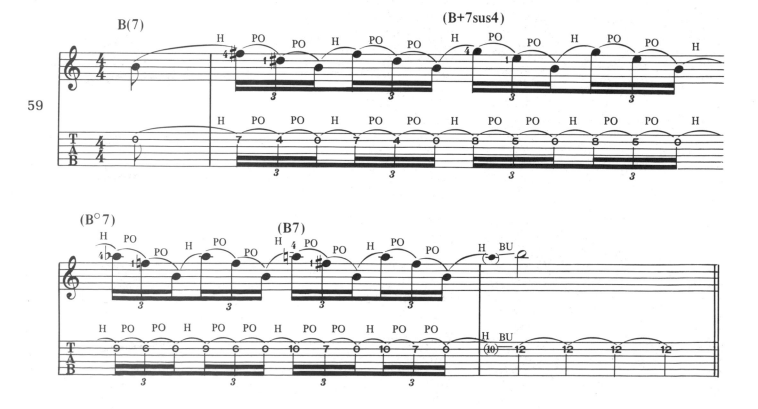

54

To hear a riff like the following one, listen to Rush's "YYZ" from their album *Exit Stage Left.*

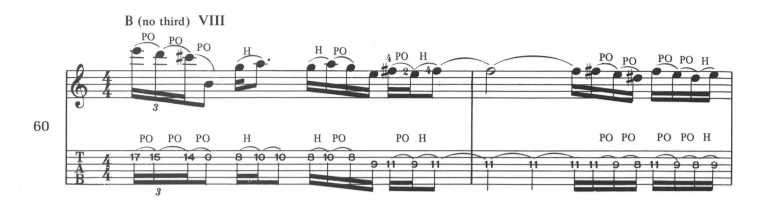

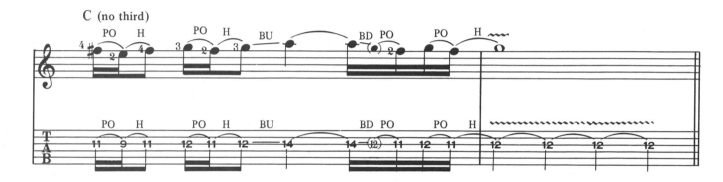

Listen to the solo on the Scorpions' title cut "Blackout" to hear a riff just like this one.

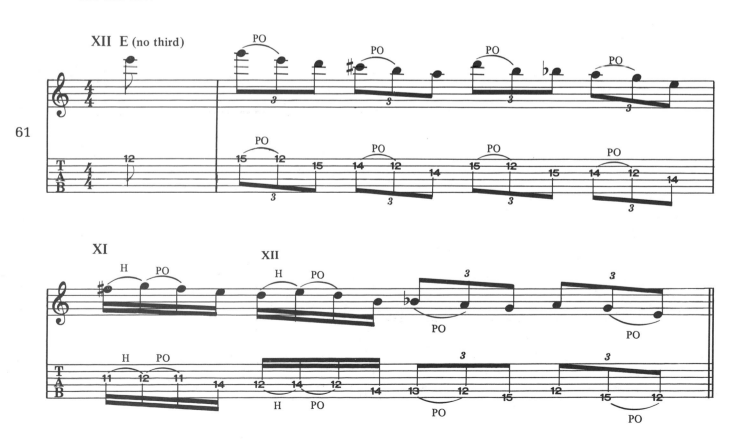

Angus Young

Wearing an Australian schoolboy's uniform and pounding out megadecibel leads on one of his variously dated Gibson SGs (he owns over fifteen of them) is the trademark of Angus Young, lead guitarist for Australia's AC/DC. Young was born in Scotland, but his family relocated to Australia in 1964. Young's first introduction to Rock and Roll came from his oldest sister, Margaret, who played him 78s of Elvis Presley, Fats Domino, and Chuck Berry in the mid fifties. Shortly after moving to Australia Angus's older brother, Alex, formed a band called the Easybeats who precipitated Australia's equivalent of Beatlemania. The success of the Easybeats caused grade schoolers Angus and brother Malcolm (rhythm guitarist for AC/DC and five years Angus's senior) to sit up and take notice of the serious possibilities Rock and Roll had to offer. The Easybeats relocated to England and older brother Alex began sending his younger brothers records by the likes of the Beatles, Rolling Stones, John Mayall's Bluesbreakers with Eric Clapton, and Paul Butterfield. After a series of day jobs and teen bands AC/DC was formed, named by Margaret from an inscription on the family vacuum cleaner.

AC/DC was very successful in Australia for at least two years before they signed a worldwide recording contract with Atlantic. AC/DC, like the Easybeats, relocated to England where they quickly amassed a huge following. Lead singer Bon Scott died of alcohol abuse and was replaced by leather-throated Englishman Brian Johnson, who contributed heavily to 1980's *Back in Black* LP.

Angus uses no signal-processing effects but has used the Schaeffer-Vega wireless system since 1977. His four 100-watt Marshall stacks have been doctored to resemble the old, pre-master-volume Marshalls. He keeps the volume on full but the treble, midrange, and bass controls at half and presence at zero. His amp of choice in the studio is an old 50-watt Marshall. He uses a heavy-gauge Fender pick and Gibson strings (.009, .011, .016, .024, .032, .042).

Angus Young considers his playing in AC/DC to be color on top of brother Malcolm's rhythm-guitar work, although both agree that they rarely exchange musical ideas. One of the advantages of siblings playing together in a band is that they feel free to criticize and communicate with each other without being wary of stepping on each other's toes. Angus's solos are masterful and creative and are characterized by a wide, sweeping, finger vibrato. He is always the master showman, and more often than not the center of attention riding the shoulders of lead singer Brian Johnson.

Advanced Eighth-Note and Sixteenth-Note Riffs

Quiet Riot's "Cum On Feel the Noize" features Carlos Cavazo playing a riff such as the following:

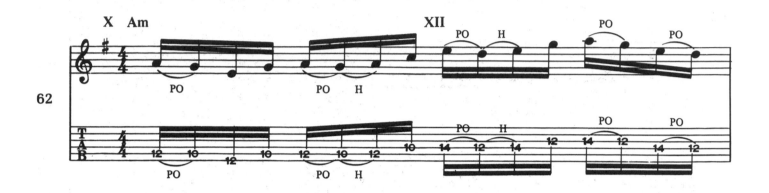

62

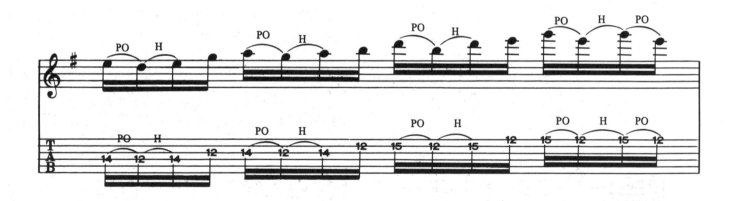

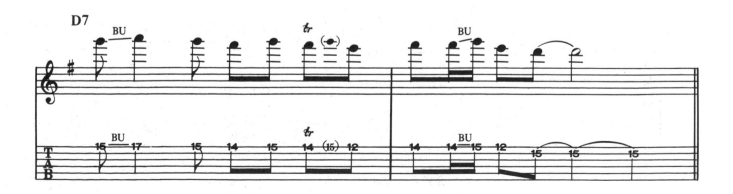

58

Listen to David Gilmour's playing on Pink Floyd's "Brain Damage" to get an idea of how this riff sounds. Notice how he forces the F♯ against the G⁷ chord in the second measure.

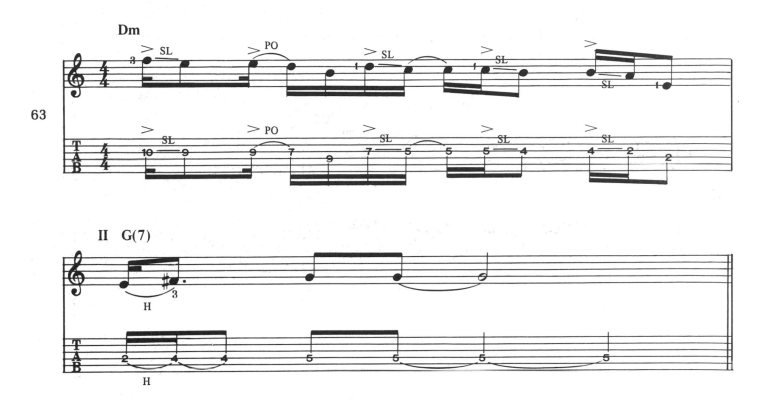

You can play the last measure here without benefit of a vibrato bar; just slide down to the F♯ and back up to the G. Refer to Def Leppard's "Comin' Under Fire."

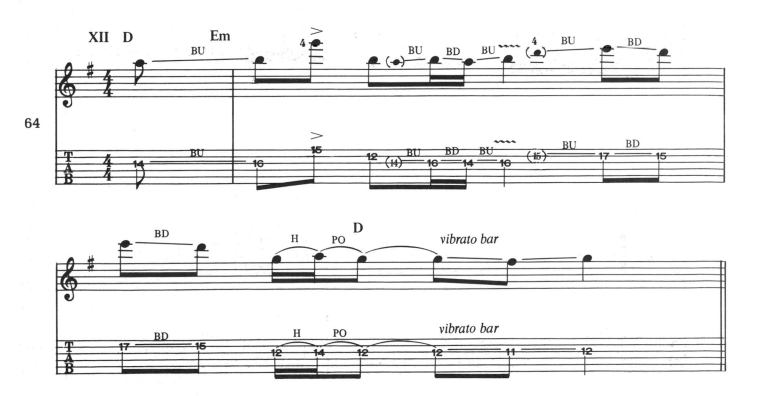

You can hear a riff like this on Iron Maiden's *Piece of Mind*.

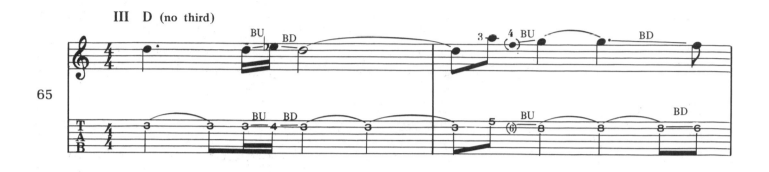

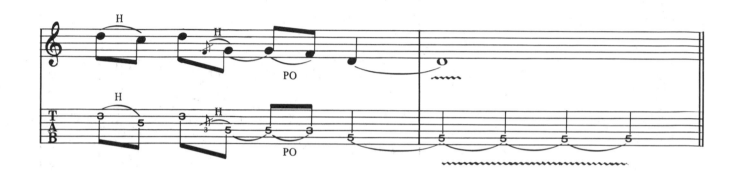

Def Leppard's "Mirror Mirror" features a riff like this one.

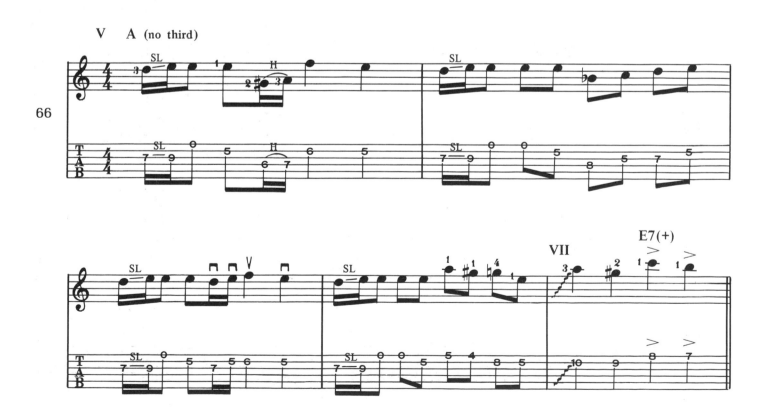

Check out Quiet Riot's "Love's a Bitch" to hear a riff very much like this one:

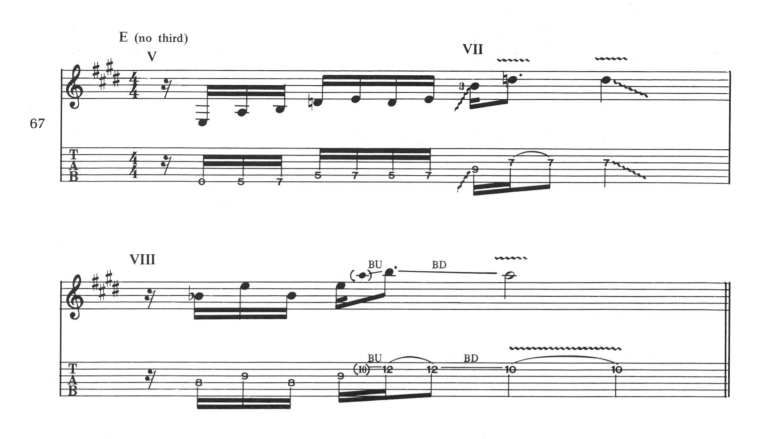

To hear a riff like the following one, listen to the Scorpions' "China White" from *Blackout*.

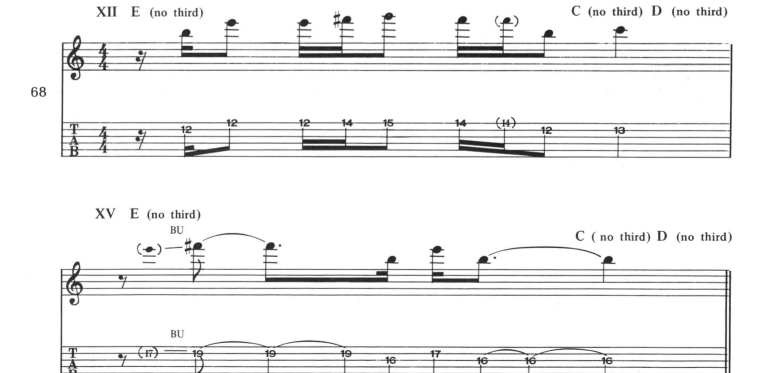

This riff is played at a slow ⁴⁄₄ tempo with a halftime feel. It may be repeated over various chords in the key of A major. Listen to the Scorpions' "Sunday Morning."

The last two beats of the first two measures here feature a motif based on fourths. Refer to "Ridin' on the Wind" by Judas Priest.

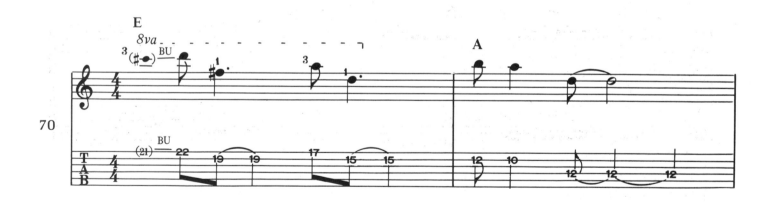

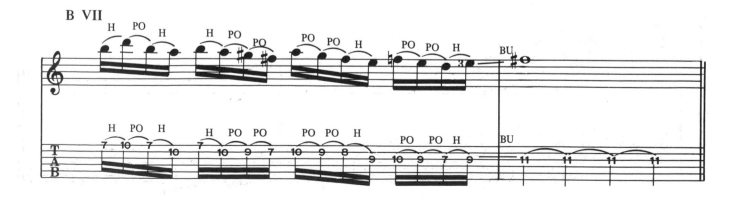

62

This riff lays out a beautiful melodic motif, first in A and then in G. Listen to Van Halen's "Runnin' with the Devil."

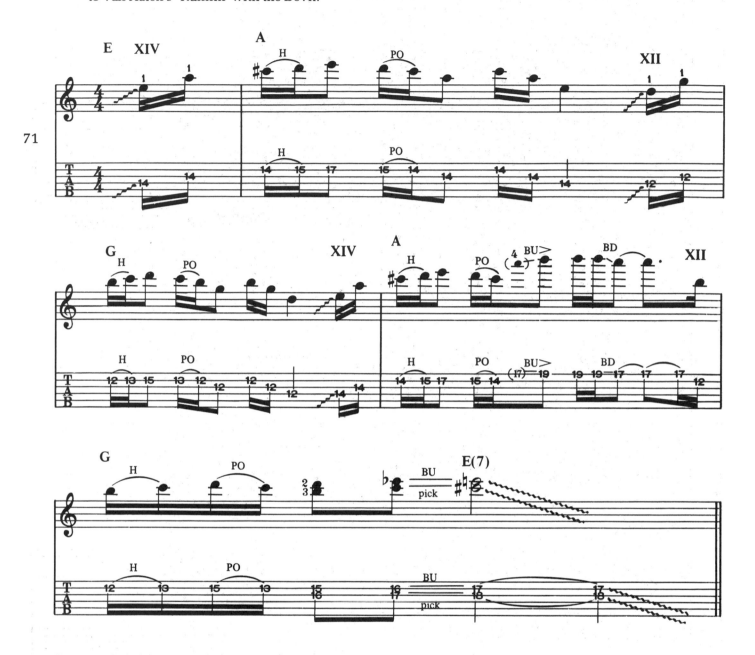

You'll need to be using extra-light gauge strings to easily execute the bends in this riff. Check out Van Halen's solo in "You Really Got Me" to hear a riff like this one.

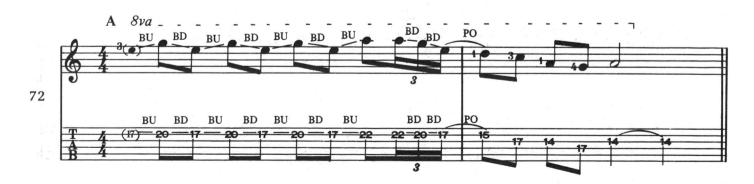

A high note juxtaposed against a low one is an effective, earcatching device. That's how this riff starts out. Refer to REO's "Keep Takin' Those Back Roads" from their *Tuna Fish* album.

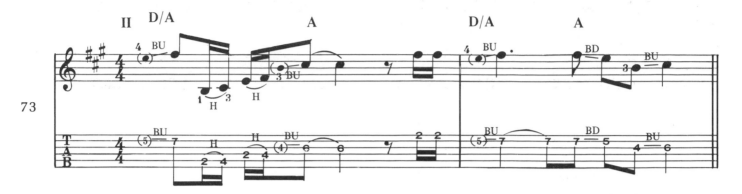

Def Leppard's hit song "Photograph" features a riff similar to this one.

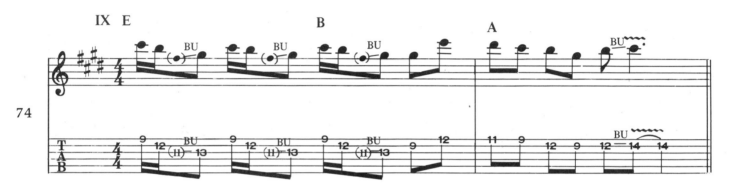

Notice the Ab here against the Am chord (it's okay). This riff is in the style of Steve Clark of Def Leppard. Listen to "Stage Fright" from *Pyromania*.

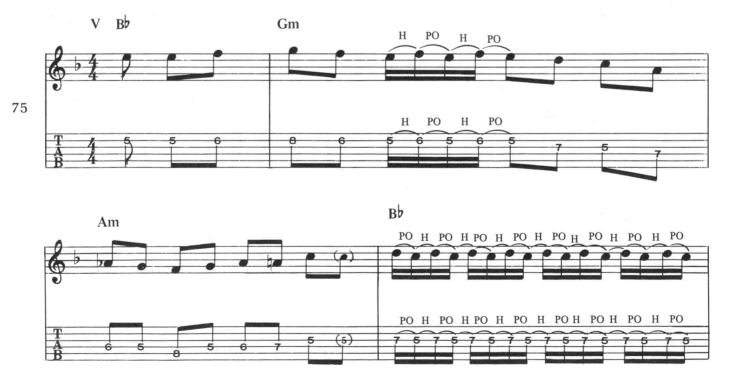

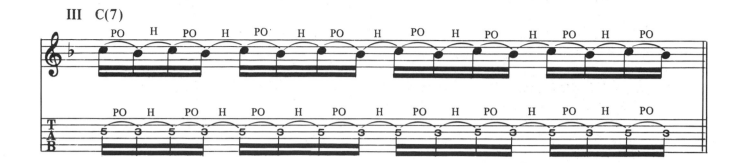

This riff is reminiscent of what is played by Gary Richrath in REO's "Keep On Lovin' You."

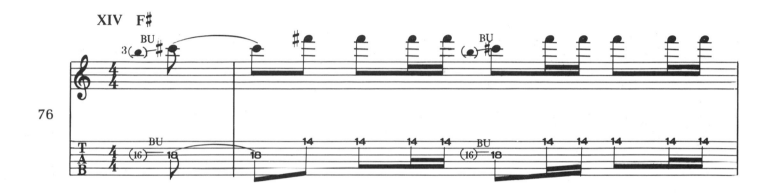

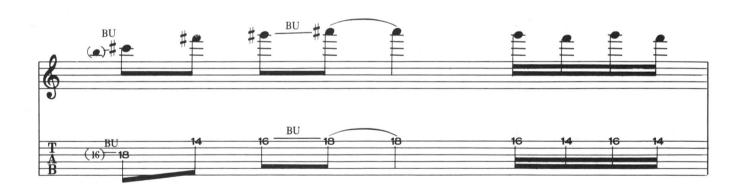

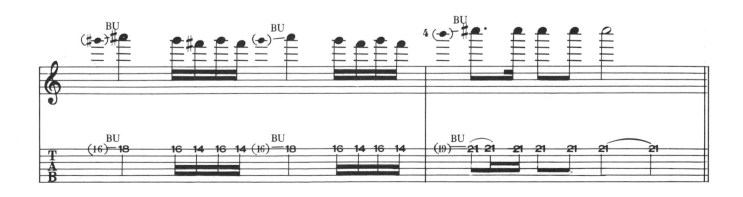

Steve Clark and Joe Elliot of Def Leppard

Carlos Cavazo of Quiet Riot plays a riff like this one in "Metal Health," which has a halftime feel to it.

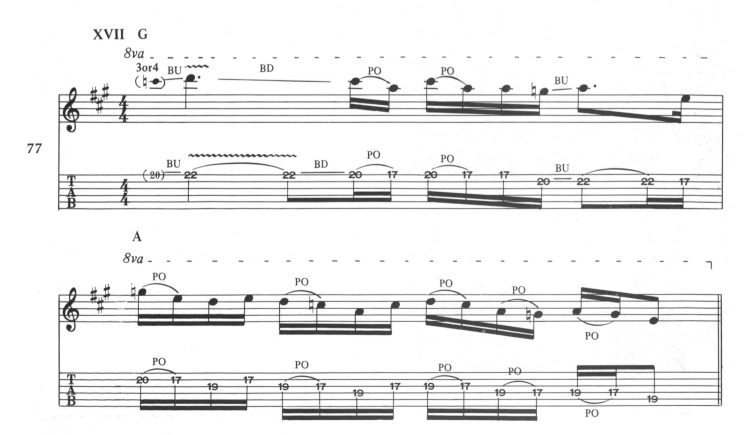

66

Gary Richrath

A playing vocabulary that blends speed and melodic riffing with unusual sounds is the trademark of REO's Gary Richrath. Like many of his influences—Jeff Beck, Jimmy Page, Peter Townshend, and Billy Gibbons—Richrath utilizes chirps, melodic riffing, harmonics, circle picking, and speed to constantly expand the creative aspects of his playing. Richrath claims his style developed in bars, where it was necessary to constantly play fast and stay in the upper register just to be heard.

Today Gary uses a 1960 Gibson Les Paul and (guess what) a Marshall amp. An exceptional trait of Richrath's is the fact that he uses no electronic effects—especially unusual when you consider that he is the band's producer.

Richrath begins building a solo by keying in on the vocal melody. From there he utilizes his repertoire of various playing techniques to produce an interesting and structured solo. It's not easy building a unique solo but constantly expanding your playing vocabulary gives you a creative edge over monotone.

Richrath's style has developed proportionately with the release of each of REO's albums. The band is extremely popular in the US—witness the success of multiplatinum *Hi Infidelity*, Billboard magazine's top seller for 1981 and one of CBS Records' biggest selling LPs ever. Richrath's role as producer/guitarist/songwriter forces him to constantly improve and expand both his guitar playing and production skills and to keep both current in the ever-changing world of popular music.

High-Note Riffs

Glenn Tipton of Judas Priest plays something like the following on "You Got Another Thing Comin'."

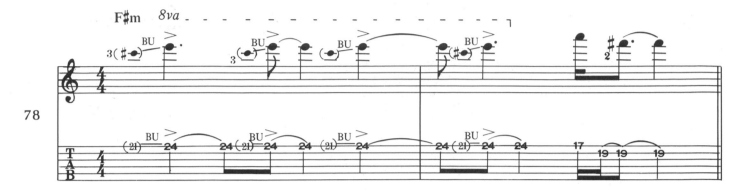

This riff is very straightforward; refer to REO's "Don't Let Him Go."

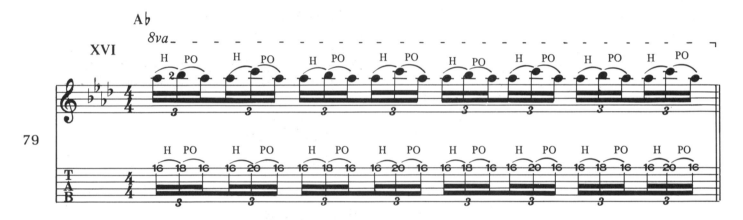

Two views of David Gilmour: 1978 and today

Here's another riff in the style of Gary Richrath of REO. Listen to their song "Take It on the Run."

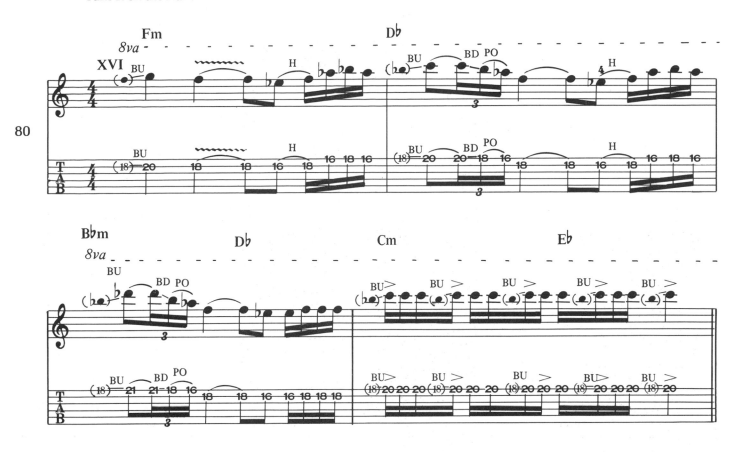

In AC/DC's "Hell's Bells" you'll hear Angus Young play riffs like the following two. He gets the most out of the blues scale.

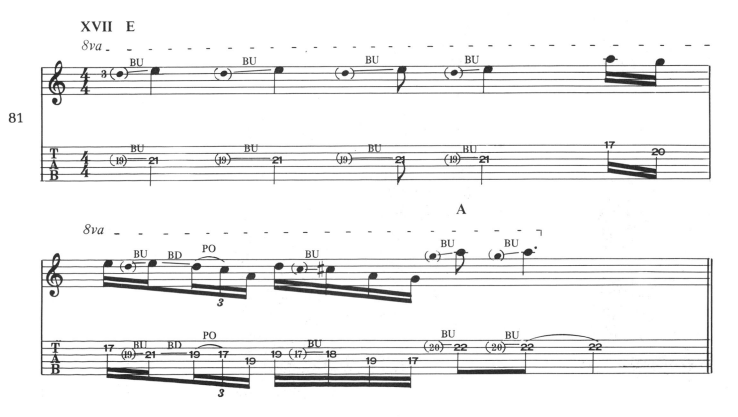

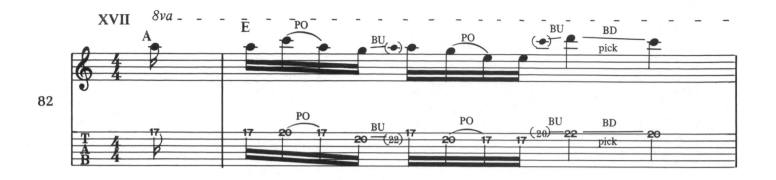

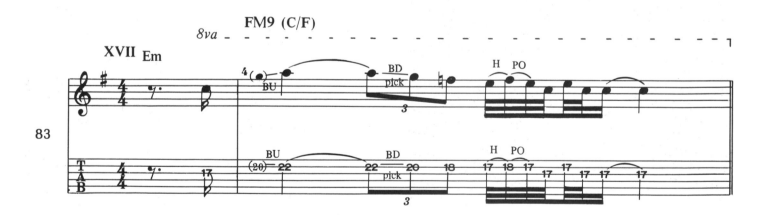

The next riff is reminiscent of the playing of David Gilmour. Check out his solo album.

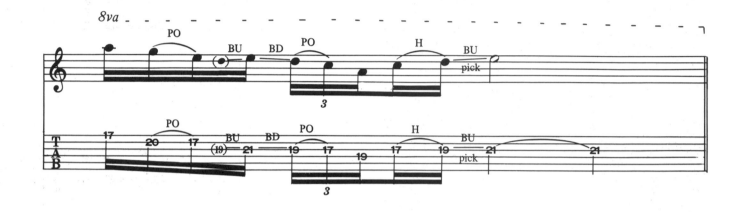

To hear a riff like this one played properly, listen to Def Leppard's "Rock!
Rock! (Till You Drop)."

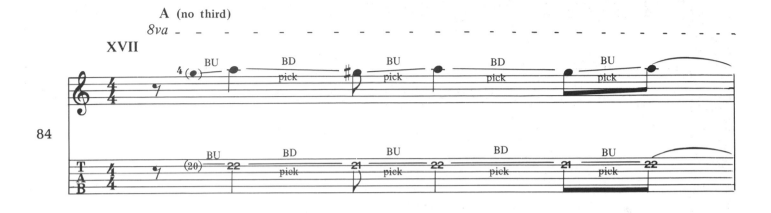

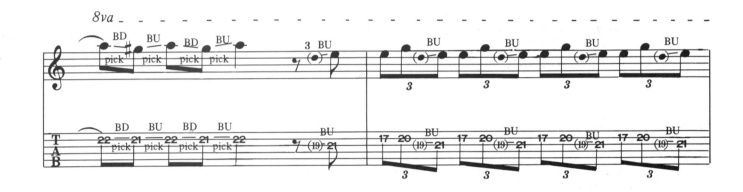

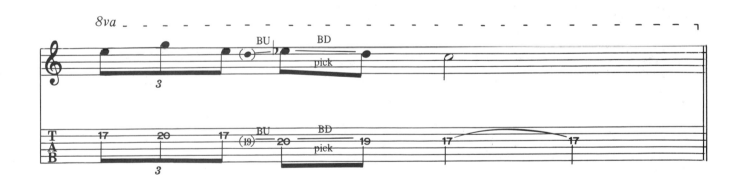

Don't worry if you don't have a vibrato bar; slide down from the F♯ to the
F♮. Refer to Iron Maiden's "The Trooper."

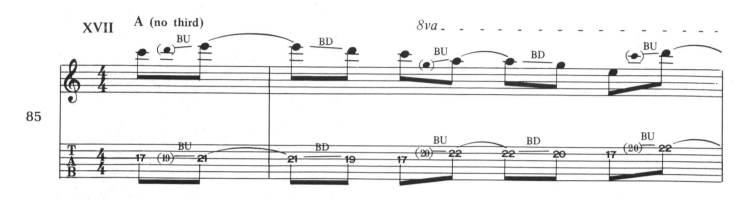

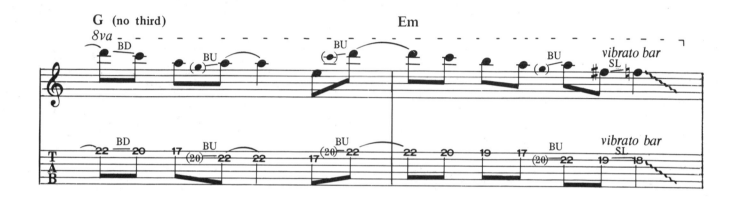

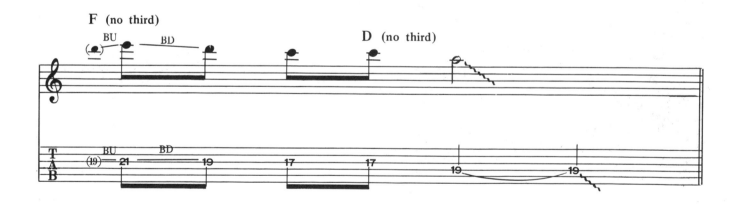

David Gilmour uses great phrasing in his simple, bluesy licks. Listen to the end of "Money" on Pink Floyd's *Dark Side of the Moon* to hear something like the following. Your guitar must have twenty-one frets for this one.

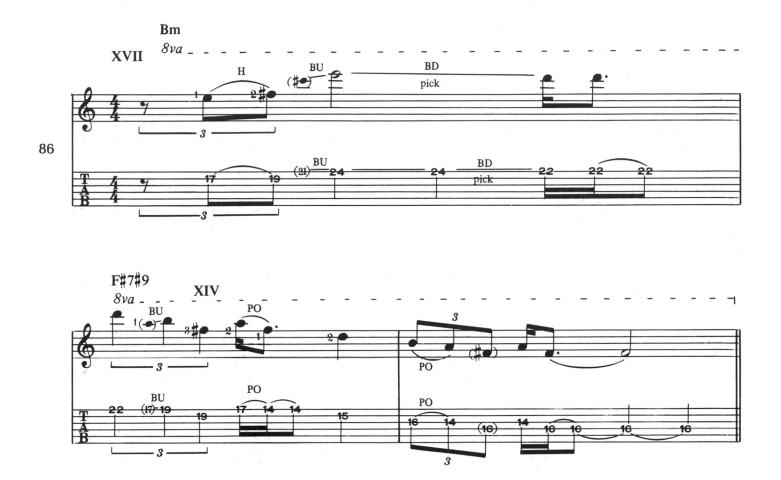

Here's a lick using the blues (pentatonic) scale against an A chord. Listen to the end of the solo on the Scorpions' "Now!"

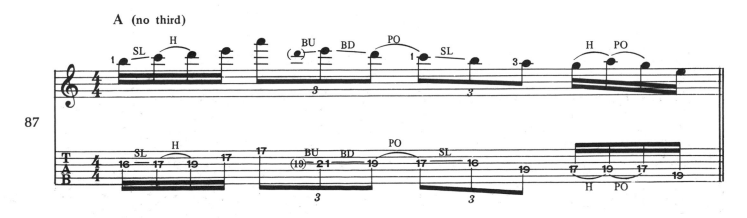

Matthias Jabs and Rudolf Schenker of the Scorpions

Another mock-Scorpion riff; this time refer to "Arizona." Don't let the thirty-second notes scare you—they are nothing but quick hammeron/pulloff sequences.

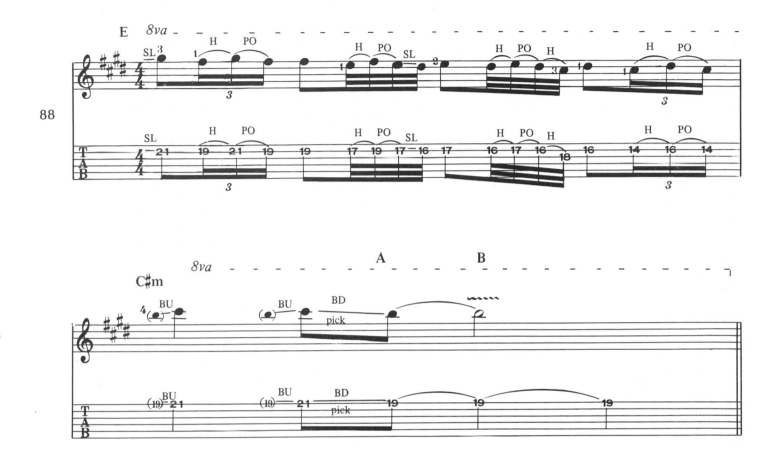

This simple lick is included because the accent is put on the third beat with the shake on the C note. It is very effective. Listen to Gary Moore on "Wishing Well" (from *Corridors of Power*).

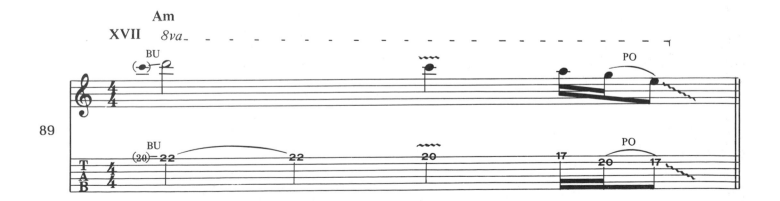

Special Solo Section:
Ozzy Osborne's "Diary of a Madman"

Playing in ⁷⁄₄ time, the late Randy Rhoads really shows his stuff on Ozzy Osbourne's "Diary of a Madman" from the album of the same name. This solo is similar to that great effort. Pay particular attention to how he phrases within the mixed meter and to his use of minor and diminished scales.

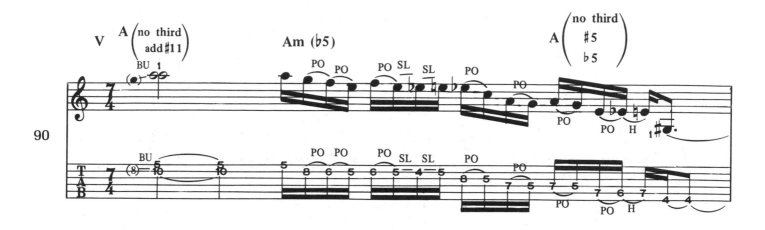

90

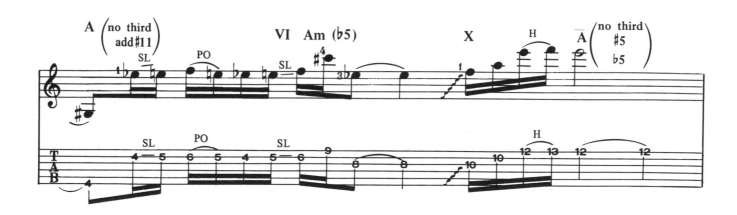

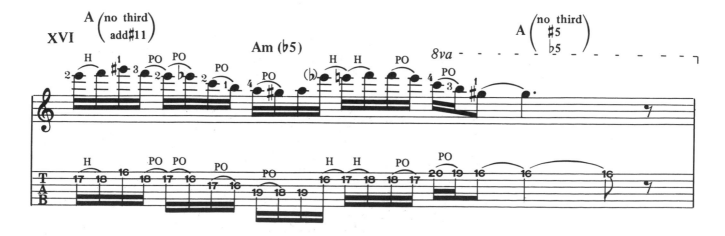

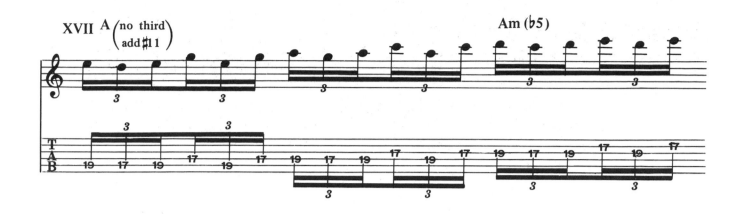

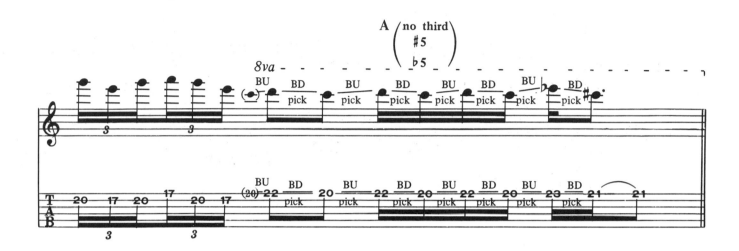

Randy Rhoads

One of the great losses of Rock and Roll was the untimely death of Randy Rhoads, who died in a plane crash in 1982 while on tour with Ozzy Osbourne. By all accounts Randy's talent would have taken him far beyond the realm of Heavy Metal and he would have eventually established himself as a guitar legend.

Rhoads was a man who truly loved to play the guitar. Born the son of two music teachers in Santa Monica, California, in 1956, Randy got his first guitar when he was six and a half. He quickly learned everything his first teacher knew. He continued to take Classical lessons off and on and, at age fourteen, started a band with his brother on drums called Violet Fox. About this time he saw Alice Cooper in concert and Randy realized that he wanted to make his career in Rock and Roll. He continued to play in high-school bands until 1977 when he was asked to join Quiet Riot. After the original Quiet Riot broke up he joined Ozzy Osbourne.

A look at Randy's broad range of influences and it becomes apparent that he was much more than a stereotypical Heavy Metal guitarist: Alan Wordsworth, Andy Summers, Pat Metheny, John McLaughlin, B.B. King, Ronnie Montrose, and Earl Klugh to name a few. These influences, as well as Rhoads's great love of Classical music, helped establish him as one of Heavy Metal's most unique players.

Randy was sometimes seen playing a Gibson Black Beauty or an SG but his favorite ax was his white Les Paul. His usual amp setup was a Peavey head into a ported Ampeg bottom.

Rhoads's approach to playing was to make the guitar a part of himself, to use it as a voice. He felt that phrasing was the most important aspect to develop in his playing. People don't speak in a monotone and Randy did not want to play in a monotone.

Ozzy Osbourne Band: Ozzy, Rudy Sarzo, Randy Rhoads, Tommy Aldridge

Unmeasured Tremolo Riffs

Unmeasured tremolo is defined as the rapid reiteration of a single note by short up- and down-strokes, producing an indefinite number of repetitions. I find that I can get the pick going at a faster, more even rate if my movement is from the arm and shoulder rather than from the wrist or finger holding the pick. Heavy Metal guitarists seem to like this technique a lot; it certainly is ear-catching and is especially effective when incorporated into a riff (see the second example below).

For the first example, check out Def Leppard's "Foolin' Around"; for the second, Def Leppard's "Action Not Words."

Bimanual (Two-Hand) Riffs

The two-handed technique associated with Eddie Van Halen's playing is something all guitarists should have within their vocabulary of riffs. Other guitarists have been using this technique for years (Randy Rhoads, Jeff Watson of Night Ranger, Rick Derringer, and myself—since 1976) but Van Halen really put his signature on it by becoming unusually adept and creative at bimanual riffs.

Some players "bury" the pick in the palm of their hand when commencing to play bimanually; some hammeron with the right index finger (*i*), some with the right middle finger (*m*) and some with the right ring finger (*a*). Jeff Watson is especially talented at an eight-finger style, utilizing four left-hand and four right-hand fingers. When I start to play bimanually, I generally discard the pick (often in my mouth—unsanitary but handy) as I prefer to do my hammering on and pulling off unencumbered by a pick.

I have included some riffs in this section which are bimanual only in the sense that you are hammering on a single note within a riff. The first three riffs below employ this technique within a riff.

I have notated these riffs in the manner in which *I* play them. You might find a variation of your own to be more comfortable. If so, *go with it!*

You've heard this particular technique before; hammering on a high note on the same string on which you have just played a lower note. Refer to Iron Maiden's "Innocent Exile" on *Killers* for the first riff and Van Halen on "You Really Got Me" for the second.

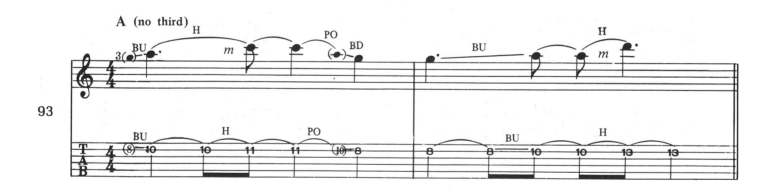

93

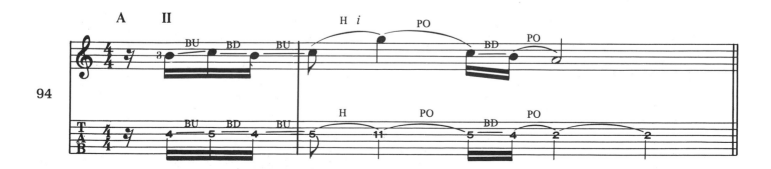

94

Dave Murray of Iron Maiden and friend

The next two riffs, reminiscent of the Scorpions' "Can't Live Without You," employ the bimanual technique within a regularly fretted and picked riff.

Okay, get ready for the real thing. This riff is highly similar to what Eddie Van Halen plays in "I'm the One." Note that the bimanual playing takes place on the second string, although it could also be done on the third string.

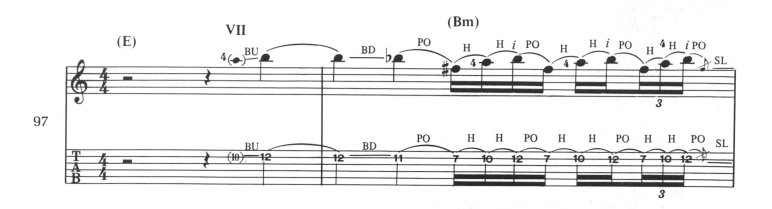

97

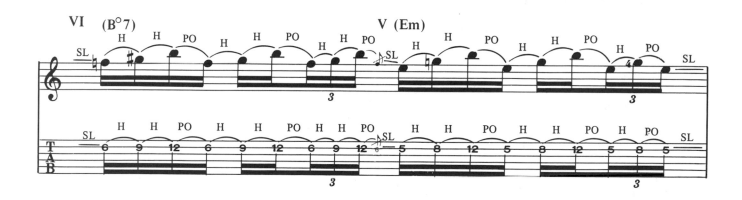

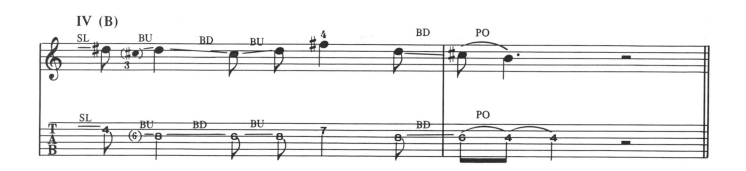

Now that you've mastered the previous riff, here's a bimanual riff combining sixteenth notes and triplets. Once again, very similar to Van Halen; this time it's like what he plays alone with the drums on "Ice Cream Man."

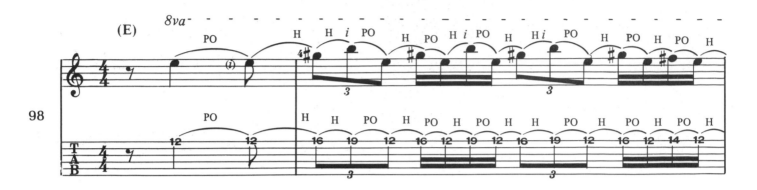

98

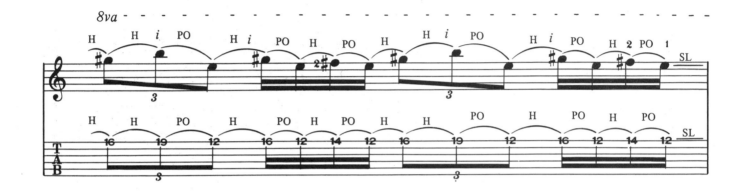

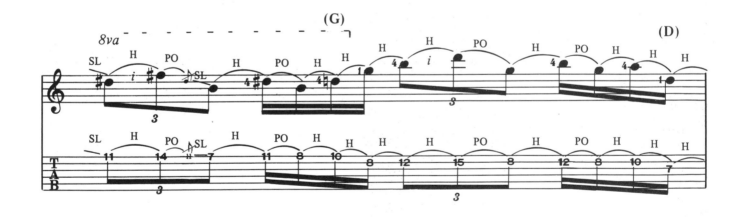

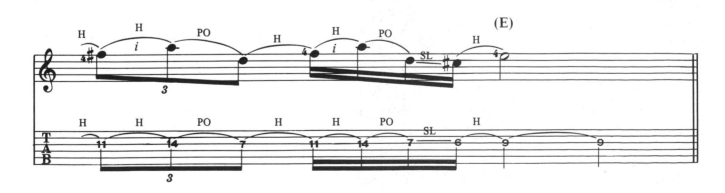

Going back to the earlier examples of two-handed playing within a regular riff, you will recognize this as being like Van Halen's playing on "Secrets."

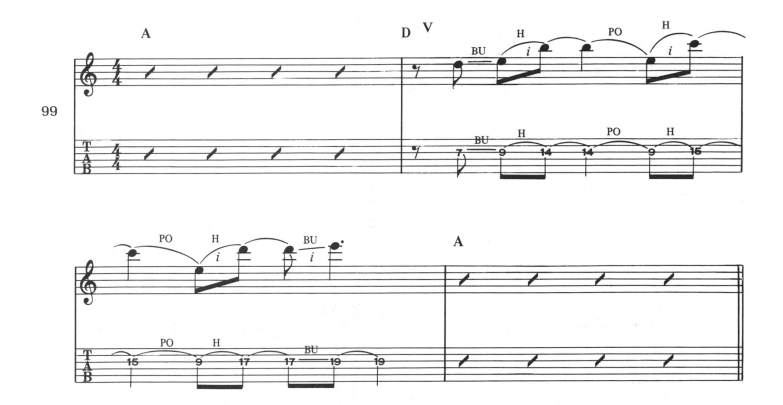

Eddie Van Halen

You'll hear Jeff Watson of Night Ranger play a lick just like this one on "Don't Tell Me You Love Me."

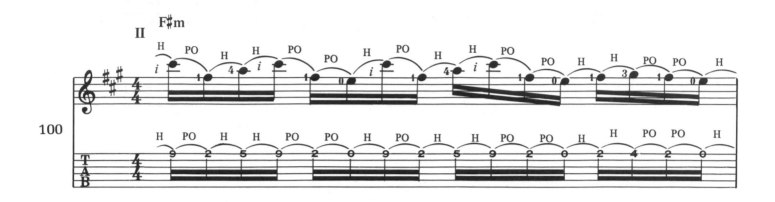

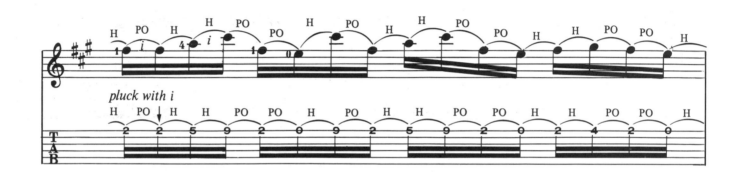

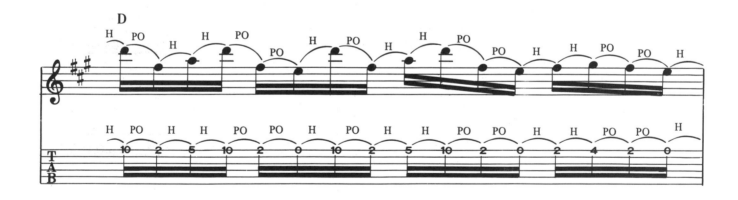

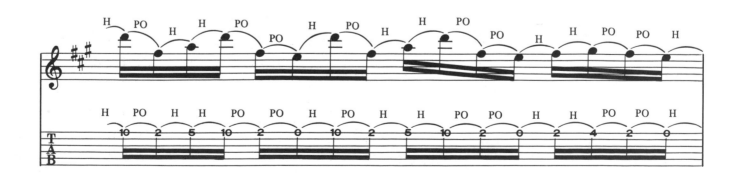

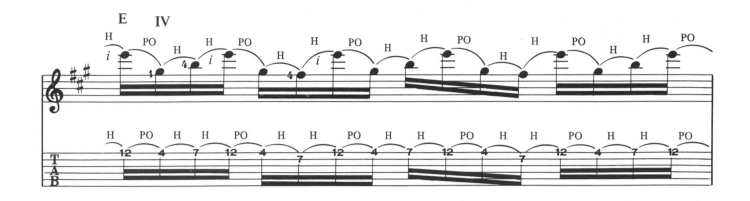

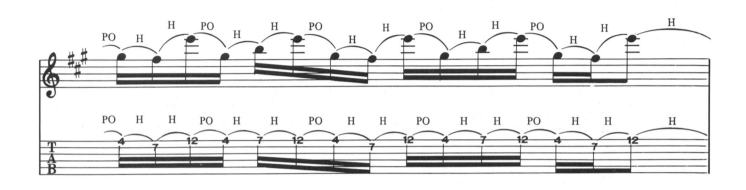

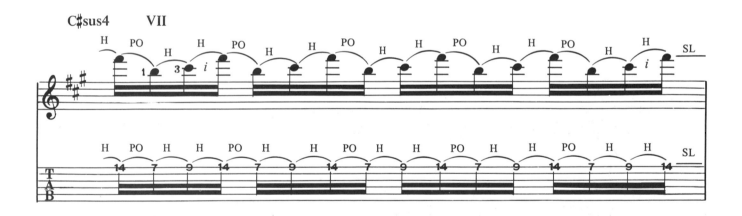

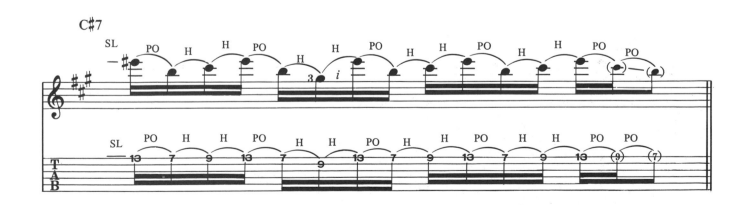

Jeff Watson/Brad Gillis

The combination of Jeff Watson and Brad Gillis as co-lead-guitarists for the band Night Ranger makes for some extraordinary musicianship. Each guitarist is able to feed the other inspiration and ideas; a unique arrangement in a business otherwise known for its cutthroat competition. The variations in their styles—Watson's blazing fast, fluid lines as opposed to Gillis's tremolo-bar approach—cause Night Ranger to be a musically more interesting band, concentrating on musicianship as well as attitude.

Jeff Watson, twenty-seven, has played the guitar for twenty years. He polished his speed chops by playing his battered Yamaha twelve-string in Sacramento, California high-school bands and copping licks from Johnny Winter, Shuggie Otis, Eddie Van Halen, Neal Schon, and Ronnie Montrose. When he was eighteen he joined Sammy Hagar's Band and went from there to forming his own band. In 1979, Night Ranger was formed and keyboardist Alan Fitzgerald, who had produced demos for the Jeff Watson Group, brought Jeff Watson on board as guitarist.

Jeff's 1956 Goldtop Gibson Les Paul has been routed out to accomodate a DiMarzio SD pickup in back and a Gibson Dirty Fingers pickup in front. His affinity for chrome extends beyond the hardware on his ax to the chrome pick he features. In the studio Watson goes through a beefed-up preamp into a 100-watt Hi-Watt amp. Live, he uses the Nady wireless system into a solid-state Projector Series for lead work and a Marshall for rhythm parts. The most prominent feature of his effects setup is his rack-mounted Roland RE-555 chorus/echo.

Brad Gillis, twenty-six, was born in Hawaii and began playing guitar at age eight. His early influences included the Beatles, Ritchie Blackmore, and Jimmy Page. After he graduated from high school he played out five nights a week with a Top 40 band called Arm & Hammer, an experience he claims broke him out of the traditional Rock and Roll riff mode and into a more rhythmic approach to playing. At nineteen he did his first recording with a Funk band called Rubicon. When the recording flopped Gillis went to San Francisco and formed a New Wave band, Stereo. In 1979, he formed Night Ranger, and in 1981, while waiting for Night Ranger to hit, did some gigs as Randy Rhoads's replacement with Ozzy Osbourne.

The guitar you will most often see Gillis playing is his red 1962 Strat with a Mighty Mite body, Seymour Duncan J.B. pickups, and a twenty-second fret added on. All of his guitars are equipped with the Floyd Rose tremolo system and he uses GHS strings. Like Jeff Watson, his signal goes through the Nady wireless system. From there it passes through a PCM A1 Lexicon and an ADA stereo tape-delay into two Mesa Boogie amps.

Jeff Watson/Brad Gillis

Brad Gillis

Jeff Watson

Chromatic and Diminished Riffs

The most commonly heard application of a diminished arpeggio in rock and blues is over a chord of the same name; for example, A°7 against an A chord. Refer to Def Leppard's "Satellite" for this riff.

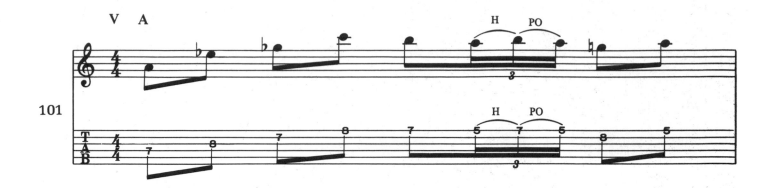

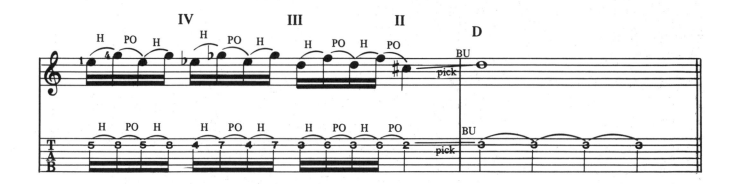

Here's an example of a C#°7 chord sounding great with a C7 chord underneath. Listen to Judas Priest's "Electric Eye."

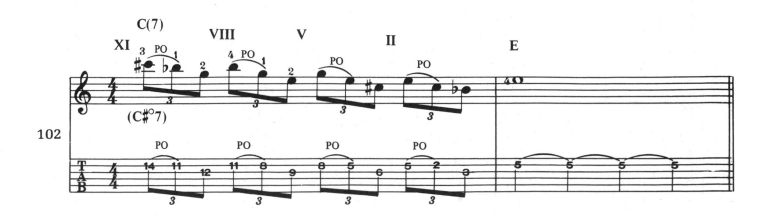

Jake E. Lee with Ozzy Osbourne

The opening statement in Randy Rhoads's solo in "Little Dolls" contains a chromatic bend such as in the following riff.

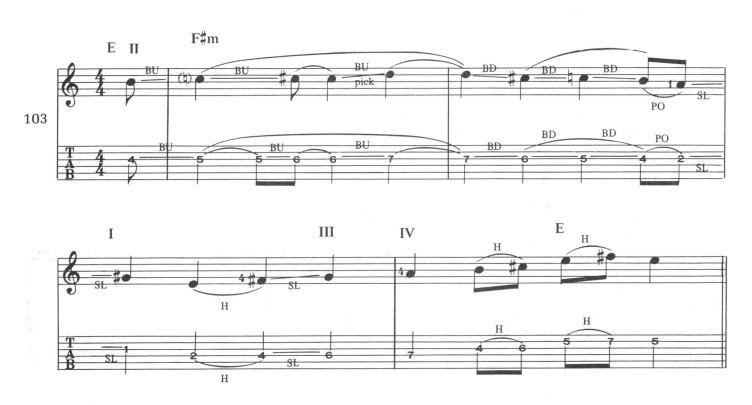

Listen to Def Leppard's "Rocks Off" to hear a chromatic riff like this one.

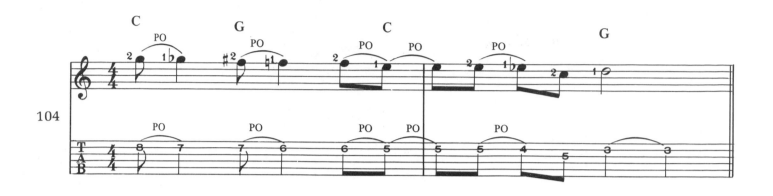

104

The D° arpeggio is used against the D (no third) chord in the second beat of the second measure below. Check out Randy's solo in Ozzy Osbourne's "Tonight" (from *Diary of a Madman*).

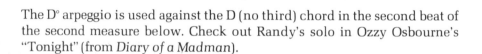

105

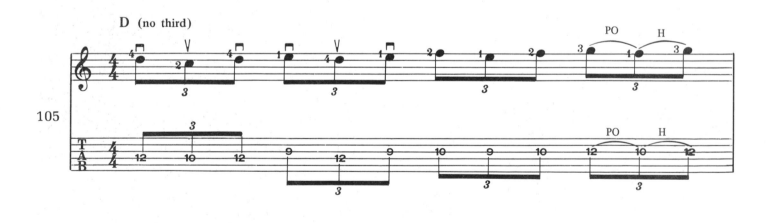

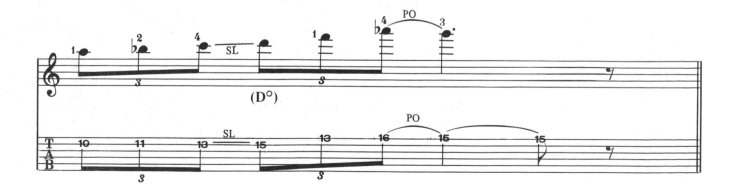

Check out this simple use of chromatics, as in Pink Floyd's "Dogs."

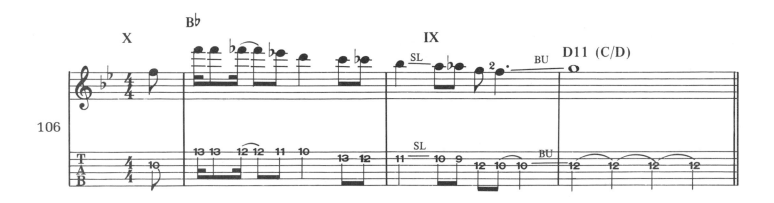

David Gilmour

Neil Geraldo

In the next riff, the hammeron/pulloff riff is moved down chromatically. Refer to Neil Geraldo's solo in "Promises in the Dark."

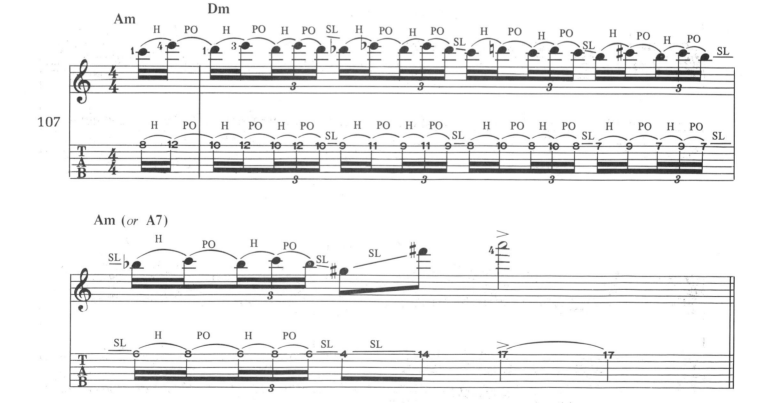

94

The last riff in this section comes from the Van Halen school of chromatics; the scale work here is quite accurate—notice which notes from the E chord are sharped or flatted as you go up the neck.

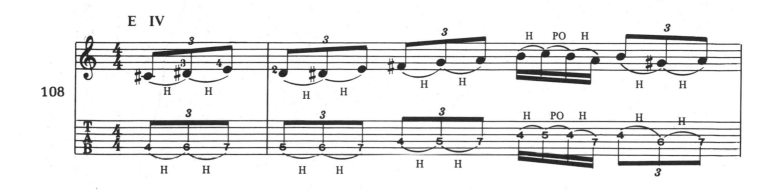

108

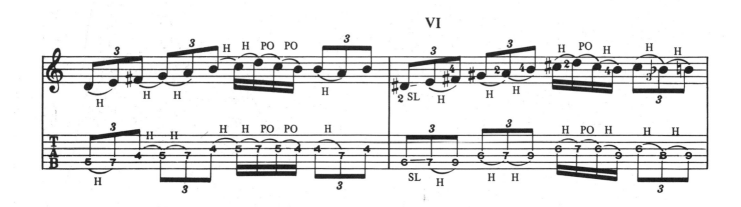

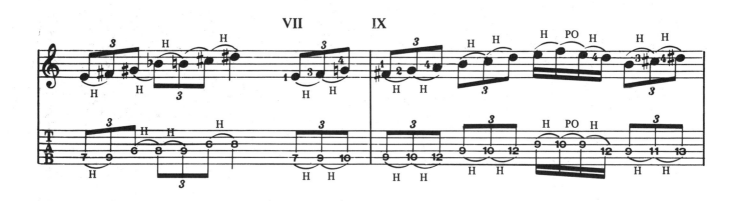

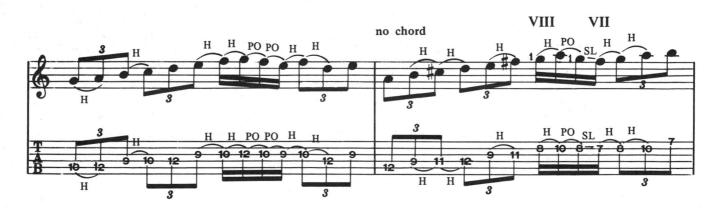

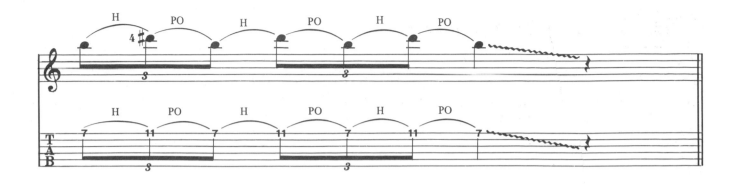

Neil Geraldo and Pat Benatar

Riffs Using Harmonics

Natural harmonics occur at various positions along the fretboard. Neil Geraldo (of Pat Benatar's band) uses them in "Precious Time," from which the next riff takes its inspiration.

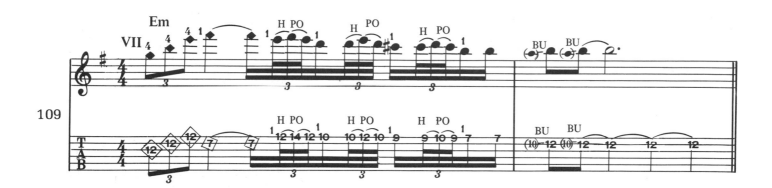

Artificial harmonics may be achieved by striking the string with the side of the pick, or a fingernail, twelve frets above the fretting finger. Refer to Van Halen's "Hang 'Em High" to hear how this riff might sound.

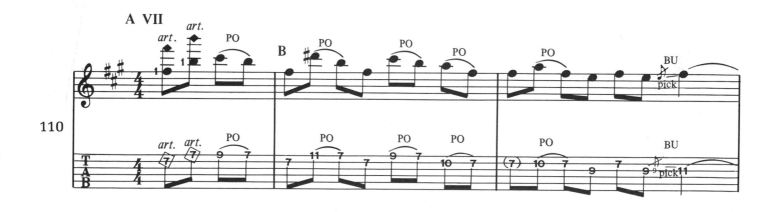

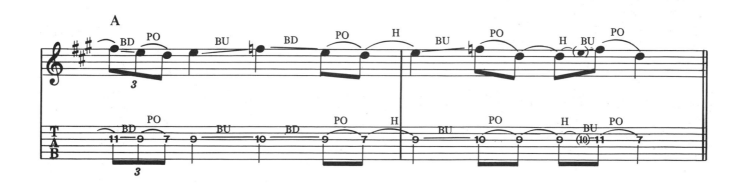

Steve Clark

Def Leppard is a very different kind of Heavy Metal band and Steve Clark mirrors the differences. Born in Sheffield, England in 1960, Clark affects a more moderate lifestyle than is flaunted by other Heavy Metal guitar players. For example, Clark prefers tennis, soccer, and golf to the Heavy Metal cliché of partying all night. Def Leppard is, after all, a band that relies on musicianship, good looks, and positive attitude to get their point across.

Def Leppard (originally known as Atomic Mass) released their first, self-produced EP, *On Through the Night*, in 1979. It was this extremely Pop effort that resulted in their signing with Phonogram in 1980.

Clark's subtle guitar style is composed of refined melodic touches, phased single-string passages, six- and twelve-string acoustic phasings, octave lines, and bluesy wah-wah leads. Much of Steve's style is reflective of his influences—studying Classical music for two years before discovering Led Zeppelin, Thin Lizzy, and T. Rex. Solos that are within the style of the tune itself as opposed to individual musicianship and flash are Clark's aim. Clark believes in practicing a lot and that much time should be devoted to music, especially in light of the fact that touring acts continue to get bigger and better.

Steve's three main axes are a cherry sunburst 1966 Les Paul Deluxe, a 1975 Les Paul Standard, and a Les Paul XR-1. He employs a Boss chorus, a Boss delay unit, and a Morley volume booster, but uses each of them sparingly.

Def Leppard

Phil Collen and Steve Clark

Muted Riffs

Both these examples show muting with the palm of the right hand. Listen to the playing of Def Leppard to get a good idea of this technique, especially "You Got Me Runnin' " and "Lady Strange."

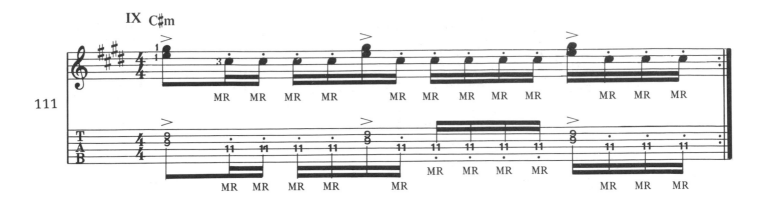

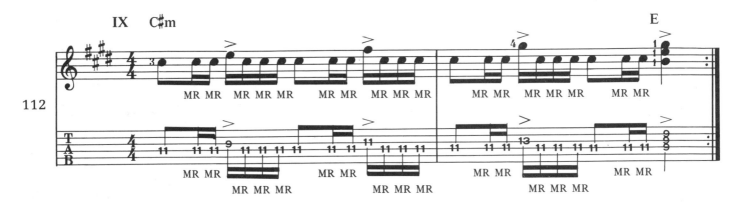

Scorpions

Bitonal Riffs

Alex Lifeson of Rush is quite adept at imposing one major chord over another, the difference in keys being perceived as dissonance. Refer to "Xanadu," from *Exit Stage Left*.

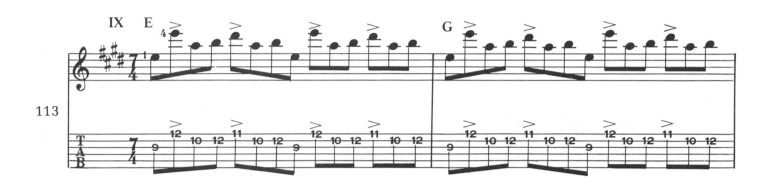

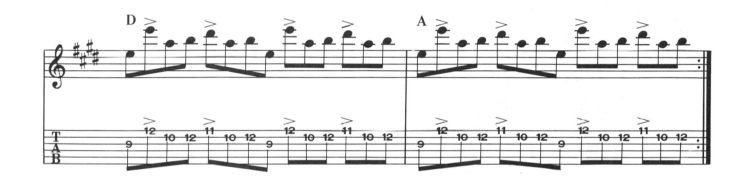

An E Major chord is arpeggiated against an A chord in this riff, highly similar to what is played in Def Leppard's "Answer to the Master."

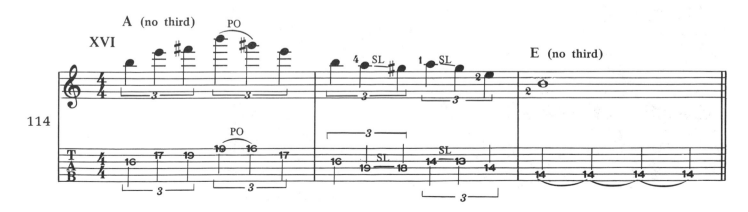

Trilled Riffs

One usually trills a note with the next higher note in the diatonic scale.
The first trill below is different. Listen to Iron Maiden's "Die with Your
Boots On."

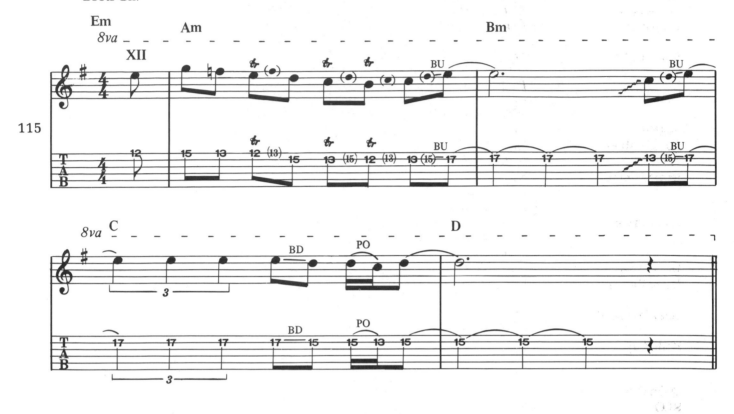

Here again, the riff is in G major but the last trill in the second measure is E
to F♮ instead of E to F♯. Refer to Iron Maiden's "Sun and Steel" from *Piece
of Mind*.

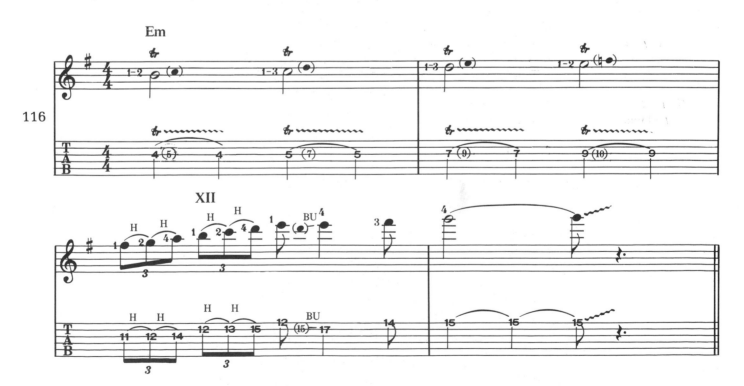

DISCOGRAPHY

AC/DC	Back in Black	Atlantic SD-16018
Pat Benatar	Precious Time	Chrysalis CHR 1346
Deep Purple	Burn	Warner Brothers 2768
Def Leppard	On Through the Night	Mercury SRM-1-3828
	High n' Dry	Mercury SRM-1-4021
	Pyromania	Mercury 810-308-1
Foghat	Live!	Bearsville BRK 6791
David Gilmour	David Gilmour (solo album)	Columbia JC-35388
Iron Maiden	Killers	Harvest ST-12141
	Number of the Beast	Capitol SEX-12215
	Piece of Mind	Capitol ST-12274
Judas Priest	Hell Bent for Leather	Columbia JC-35706
	Unleashed in the East	Columbia JC-36179
	Screaming for Vengeance	Columbia FC 38160
Gary Moore	Corridors of Power	Mirage 90077-1
Night Ranger	Dawn Patrol	Boardwalk NB-33259-1
Ozzy Osbourne	Blizzard of Oz	Jet JZ 36812
	Diary of a Madman	Jet FZ 37492
Pink Floyd	Dark Side of the Moon	Harvest SMAS 11163
	Animals	Columbia JC-34474
Quiet Riot	Metal Health	Pasha FZ-38443
REO	You Can Tune a Piano but You Can't Tuna Fish	Epic JE-35082
	Hi Infidelity	Epic FE 36844
Rush	Signals	Mercury SRM-1-4063
	Exit Stage Left	Mercury SRM-2-7001
Scorpions	Animal Magnetism	Mercury SRM-1-3825
	Blackout	Mercury SRM-1-4039
Triumph	Allied Forces	RCA AFL-1-3902
Van Halen	Van Halen (first album)	Warner Brothers 1-3075
	Van Halen II	Warner Brothers HS-3312
	Diver Down	Warner Brothers BSK 3677

Riff Cassettes Available!

by Mark Michaels

Heavy Metal Riffs for Guitar

Includes riffs in the style of AC/DC (Angus Young), Pat Benatar (Neil Geraldo), Ritchie Blackmore, Foghat, Pink Floyd (David Gilmour), Def Leppard, Iron Maiden, Gary Moore, Judas Priest, Night Ranger, Ozzy Osbourne (Randy Rhoads), REO Speedwagon, Quiet Riot, Rush (Alex Lifeson), Scorpions, Triumph (Rik Emmett) and Van Halen.

Rockabilly Riffs for Guitar

Includes riffs in the style of The Blasters (Dave Alvin), Bob Wills (Junior Barnard), Bill Haley (Fran Beecher, Danny Cidrone), The Rock and Roll Trio (Paul Burlison), James Burton, Danny Gatton, Gene Vincent (Cliff Gallup), Buddy Holly, Sleepy La Beef, Albert Lee, Grady Martin, Elvis (Scotty Moore), Carl Perkins, Chris Spedding, The Stray Cats (Brian Setzer), Link Wray and more.

New Wave Riffs for Guitar

Includes riffs in the style of A Flock of Seagulls, Adrian Belew, The Buzzcocks, Robert Fripp, The Psychedelic Furs, Dead Kennedys, Kraut, Television (Richard Lloyd, Tom Verlaine), Roxy Music (Phil Manzanera), The Pretenders, Robert Quine, Squeeze, Billy Idol (Steve Stevens), The Police (Andy Summers), Talking Heads (David Byrne), U2 (The Edge), X (Billy Zoom) and XTC.

Rock Riffs for Guitar

Includes riffs in the style of Duane Allman, Boston, David Bowie, The Cars, Elvis Costello, Dire Straits, The Eagles, Dave Edmunds, Fleetwood Mac, Foreigner, Peter Frampton, George Harrison, Heart, Jimi Hendrix, Ian Hunter, The Kinks, John Lennon, Bob Marley, Men At Work, Steve Miller, Van Morrison, Jimmy Page, The Pretenders, Prince, Queen, Steely Dan, Leslie West and more.

Blues Riffs for Guitar

Includes riffs in the style of Jeff Beck, Chuck Berry, Michael Bloomfield, Eric Clapton, Bo Diddley, Peter Green, Buddy Guy, Elmore James, Albert King, B.B. King, Freddie King, Keith Richard, Otis Rush, Kim Simmonds, Mick Taylor and Howlin' Wolf.

- Each companion tape contains *note-for-note* recordings of all the riffs in each book, presented in the *exact order* in which they appear in print.

- Featuring *full band accompaniment* for each riff, not just a single instrument.

- Count-off (1-2-3-4) included for each riff, so you can *play along* and learn faster, more effectively.